D1117849

Praise for Getting *un*STUCK

"You'll see yourself in the stories of this book!"

-Robin Bloom, broadcast journalist, Philadelphia, PA

"When we get stuck in life, we often create suffering for others as well as ourselves. Learning to free oneself from this pattern is at the heart of this book."

-Jerry Braza, Ph.D., author of
The Seeds of Love: Growing Mindful Relationships

"Anyone can get stuck. Shira Taylor Gura helps create the voice in your head, a mental strategy, to get you unstuck so you can get on with living your best authentic life."

-Lu Ann Cahn, speaker, author of *I Dare Me*

"All psychological and spiritual growth involves not just freedom *for* our self, but freedom *from* our self -- freedom from the automatic thoughts and behaviors toward which we've become largely unconscious, and which limit our joy and fulfillment in life. Shira Taylor Gura's methods are wise, gentle reminders on how to become more conscious, sane, and loving in an increasingly demanding world."

-Larry Dossey, MD, author of *ONE MIND:*
How Our Individual Mind Is Part of a Greater Consciousness and Why It Matters

"A totally new approach to mindfulness, effective even for those for whom 'be in the moment' advice has never worked!"

-Marshall Goldsmith, author of
the #1 *New York Times* bestseller
Triggers: Creating Behavior That Lasts--Becoming the Person You Want to Be.

"The S.T.U.C.K. Method is a wonderful, practical guide to utilizing mindfulness and emotional awareness to unstick yourself from destructive emotional patterns and live from a place of greater freedom and openness."

-Dr. Rabbi James Jacobson-Maisels,
founder of *Or HaLev: A Center for Jewish Spirituality and Meditation*

"What I find most powerful about this book is the element of 'O.K.', which is that of finding self-compassion."

-   Joanna F. Kleinman, LCSW,
Creator of the "Dethroning Your Inner Critic" series,
founder of *The Center For Extraordinary Relationships*

"Each of us can use The S.T.U.C.K. Method, a powerful technique to guide our thoughts and emotions, and thereby our bodies, away from unnecessary, heart pounding distress and towards mindful, health-promoting calm."

-Shoshana T. Melman, MD, pediatrician
director, *Foster Care Program; CARES Institute*

"Unique to this book is you don't feel like an expert is preaching at you, but a fellow human, who is finding her way through the personal struggles and emotions that we all feel."

-Leora Mitzner, PsyD, school psychologist

"The S.T.U.C.K. Method is wise, skillful, and practical. Most importantly, though, it offers the possibility of real change."

-Carla Naumburg, PhD, author of
*Ready, Set, Breathe: Practicing Mindfulness with Your Children for Fewer
Meltdowns and a More Peaceful Family*

"This makes for an honest, authentic, and absorbing text, in which nothing is taught that was not experienced first by the author herself."

- Dr. Nurit Novis Deutsch, psychologist,
The Department of Counseling and Human Development,
University of Haifa

"Shira Taylor Gura provides tangible takeaways on how to better respond to the inevitable stressors in life."

-Laura Putnam, MA, CEO of Motion Infusion,
author of *Workplace Wellness That Works*

"Several other do-it-yourself cognitive therapy systems exist, but Shira Tayor Gura's is particularly simple to implement and memorable. Try her approach once and I think you will be S.T.U.C.K. on it."

-Gretchen M. Reevy, PhD,
editor of *The Praeger Handbook on Stress and Coping*
author of *Encyclopedia of Emotion*

"With down-to-earth examples from her own life, Shira Taylor Gura presents a very practical tool to release us from the reflex-reactions we often regret."

-David Richo, author of *You Are Not What You Think*

"Shira Taylor Gura's self-deprecating humor is winning; her practical clarity is incisive; her core of compassion is inspiring."

-Frank Rogers, author of *Practicing Compassion*
professor of Spiritual Formation and Narrative Pedagogy
co-director of the *Center for Engaged Compassion*
at the Claremont School of Theology

"This intimate sharing inspires the reader to try out The S.T.U.C.K. Method for his or her own liberation."

-Rabbi Jeff Roth, director of *The Awakened Heart Project*

"This marvelous book's gift, The S.T.U.C.K. Method, offers us access to our mindful deeper self, transforms our experience, and enhances our existence."

-Nimrod Sheinman, BSc, ND
founder, *Israel Center for Mind-Body Medicine*,
director, *Israel Center for Mindfulness in Education*

"Shira Taylor Gura has produced an accessible and wise little book. Avoiding obscure terminology, she uses humour and everyday situations... to help us to wake up to the beauty of what is, and to bring insight and compassion into our lives."

-Dr. Graham Stew,
principal lecturer at the School of Health Sciences,
University of Brighton, UK

"With openness, compassion, and humor, Shira Taylor Gura shares her own struggles and successes along the way, offering a confident message that what has worked for her can certainly work for you, too."

-Diane Wyshogrod, PhD, licensed clinical psychologist
founder and director of
The Israeli Center for Mindfulness-Based Stress Reduction

SHIRA TAYLOR GURA

Getting *un*STUCK
Five Simple Steps
to Emotional Well-Being

SHIRA TAYLOR GURA

THREE GEMS   PUBLISHING

Getting *un*STUCK

Five Simple Steps to Emotional Well-Being

Copyright © 2016 Shira Taylor Gura

Three Gems Publishing
info@ThreeGemsPublishing.com
8121 Georgia Ave, suite 600
Silver Spring, MD 20910

Special discounts are available on quantity purchases by corporations, associations, and others.
For details, contact the publisher at the address above.

ISBN: 0692692339
ISBN-13: 978-0692692332

Library of Congress Control Number: 2016908763
Silver Spring, Maryland

Cover Design: Dune & Sky
Author Photo: Yonit Matilsky-Tsadok

To my husband, who continues to stand by me,
for better or for worse,
even when I get stuck.

And above all, to the Creator of all Things;
from Whom this project has come forth.
I am grateful to You.

SHIRA TAYLOR GURA

"Between stimulus and response there is a space.
In that space is our power to choose our response.
In our response lies our growth and our freedom."
-- attributed to Viktor Frankl, author of *Man's Search for Meaning*

"I am a student of the human condition
and I understand that feelings trump reason."
-- Dennis Prager, author of *Happiness is a Serious Problem*

"God, grant me the serenity to accept the people I cannot change,

the bravery to change the person I can,

the awareness to know it's me,

and the wisdom to use The S.T.U.C.K. Method

to help me do it simply and with compassion."

-- Shira Taylor Gura, variation of an excerpt from
"The Serenity Prayer" by Reinhold Niebuhr

SHIRA TAYLOR GURA

Getting *un*STUCK

Five Simple Steps to Emotional Well-Being

Contents

Introduction

Stuck on: We Need Some Orange Curtains

A friend invited me to her house the other day for a cup of coffee.

I love sitting in my friend's house, as the environment is cozy, welcoming, and warm.

Comparing her house to mine, I mentioned how the overall ambience of our house, specifically our living room, feels cold.

She responded, "Well, sure, your house is mostly in the blues. You need some more earthy colors to warm it up. You need to add some orange."

Yes, of course. Orange. That's what I need, I thought to myself.

The next day, I measured our windows, stopped at a home-decor store, and picked up some peach-color curtains for our living room.

I thought they would be perfect for our house, warm up the living room, and make our home feel cozier.

After dinner, I took out the curtains and walked into the living room.

My husband asked me what I was holding.

"Well, you know, I was thinking. Our living room feels a little off-balance, color-wise. I think we need some orange and ..."

"What about the red yoga mat on the floor?" he interrupted sarcastically.

Huh?

What does a yoga mat have to do with anything?

He had no idea what I was holding and yet he was behaving so negatively!

He had no idea what I was going to say, but he already knew we didn't need it.

Still, I stopped and took a deep breath.

He's triggering me again.

But I'm not going to get triggered.

Calm. Calm. Breathe...

But, I was stuck on desire for these new curtains and couldn't be interrupted.

I ignored my husband's remark and returned to checking to see if the curtains would look good in the living room.

I took the curtains out of the package and held them up to the windows.

But he continued, "We don't need curtains. Why are you being so stubborn? They'll cover up the sun and light that come through from the southern windows, which we really enjoy. And curtains don't even fit on bay windows. How do you think people are going to be able to sit there if curtains will be hanging on top of the seat?"

Humph.

My daughter, watching the scene, noticed my frustrated face.

She approached me and acknowledged my efforts. She told me she loved the curtains and she thanked me for caring about the aesthetics in our house.

I love my daughter.

My daughter's acknowledgment alerted me to something I had forgotten in my upset—that I needed to take a stop.

I left the scene.

I grabbed a notebook and walked into one of my kid's rooms.

I sat down on the bed and started to process through what just happened.

A few minutes later, my husband walked into the room and sat down next to me.

He put his arm around me and apologized.

I bet my daughter had something to do with that.

Then, he looked over at my pad and said, "What's this?"

He read out loud: *Stuck on frustration.*

"Is this about me?" he asked.

I believe he never listens, he continued to read aloud.

Which brought a smile to his face.

I believe he always interrupts.

He started to giggle.

I believe he's cheap.

"Why am I cheap? I'm not cheap!" he said.

"*I believe he doesn't care at all about, about* ... what does this say? I can't read your handwriting. Oh, *aesthetics.*"

He let out a guffaw.

Which made me laugh in return.

And together, our laughter continued.

He tried to read my chicken scratch of new perspectives I was considering taking on, but he couldn't make them out.

It didn't matter that I wrote down:

- I can consider that maybe the curtains won't look right on our bay window.
- I can consider that my desires won't always lead to happiness and that orange curtains won't necessarily make me happier.
- I can consider that I caught my husband by surprise and that most likely I can actually move on with my curtain idea, as long as I discuss it together with my husband—like partners.

... because I had already finished processing and moved on to a place of emotional well-being.

I get stuck on challenging emotional situations. Every day. And most likely, you do, too. We all do.

Have you ever stepped in dog poop?

Whether or not you have, you probably know quite well what to do when it happens:

1. Scrape off the poop from your shoe as best you can on the edge of a sidewalk.
2. Find a stick or some leaves to help facilitate the removal-of-poop process.
3. Go to the nearest sink or hose and wash off the rest.
4. Move on with your life.

But what if you step in emotional poop?

Like if a good friend screams at you out of nowhere?

Or if someone rear-ends your car on your way to driving your kids to their activities?

Or if you get locked out of the house accidentally by your spouse?

Or if you just get plain frustrated that life is not going your way?

Getting "stuck on" something describes the way we stay emotionally consumed or attached to our view of any one particular situation. We can get stuck on all kinds of emotions—fear, anger, aversion, pride, gloom, desire, or even joy. When we are stuck on something, reality is clouded and we act solely on our narrow-minded personal stories instead of from a broader place of clarity and objectivity. Considering any other possible way to believe or behave in that moment is unimaginable.

Being stuck on something is the polar opposite of mindfulness, which, according to Jon Kabat-Zinn in *Wherever You Go, There You*

Are "means paying attention in a particular way: on purpose, in the present moment, and nonjudgmentally."

When I'm stuck on something, I'm not noticing anything in the present moment, and I'm very often judging others or myself. And more often than not, I'm attached to a particular emotion. I can't or won't let it go.

The truth is, when I get stuck on something, I'm often not even aware of it at first. Reality is blurred and I can see only my view. Therefore, I cannot grasp there is any other way of thinking or acting in that particular moment. And that's a pretty big problem—because I care about how I function in this world and how my behavior affects me and the people around me.

When I'm stuck on something and can only see one way of being, one path, I limit myself and the possibilities that exist in that moment. I stick to my beliefs as seen through the narrow lens of that emotion and do not open up to other perspectives. I inadvertently shut down all opportunities for self-growth and healing.

It was for these challenging emotional situations that I developed The S.T.U.C.K. Method. Using this method allows me to let go of my attachment to those emotions, expand my view, and choose different, more beneficial paths.

The S.T.U.C.K. Method provides an effective structure to process through the murkiness of everyday emotions. It constructively empowers me to become present, reflect on my beliefs, and consider additional ways of viewing life's situations. Taking on a new perspective is what ultimately transforms a sticky situation to one that is less difficult, and even improves my future.

When you've finished this book, you'll have what you need to get unstuck:

- **You'll see the many ways people get stuck—and you may recognize yourself in some**

- **You'll understand how you can implement The S.T.U.C.K. Method to promote emotional well-being.** The S.T.U.C.K. Method steps are easy to remember and you can go through them anywhere, in writing, or even in your mind; with someone else if you choose, or on your own.

- **You'll get lots of practice through following stories and completing simple worksheet pages.** The S.T.U.C.K. Method guides you toward identifying your emotions, checking the accuracy of your beliefs, broadening your perspective, and holding yourself in compassion. The S.T.U.C.K. Method works on resolving conflicts that have already occurred, as well as helping prevent conflicts from arising.

- **You'll explore how you can bring meaning to your own "stuck" experiences**.

Employing and practicing The S.T.U.C.K. Method promotes emotional well-being in my life, every day.

I hope one day it does the same for you.

Shira Taylor Gura, 2016

www.thestuckmethod.com

SHIRA TAYLOR GURA

Part I: Behind The S.T.U.C.K. Method

Imagine your typical day. You wake up, make your morning coffee, check your email, maybe get the kids off to school, or go to work. Everything is going as planned.

But then, something happens. You get triggered. You hear or see something that sets you off. This trigger may not be new to you. In fact, you may have been triggered by this same thing just a day before.

What's happening here? Both a thought and an emotion instantaneously and unconsciously arise in your mind. Psychologists, neuroscientists, and philosophers have long argued whether thought precedes emotion or emotion precedes thought. For instance, imagine you are on a walk in the woods and you suddenly spot a snake on the ground. (Actually, it is a rope, but you've mistaken it for a snake.) Which arises first, the thought ("The snake is going to hurt me!") or the emotion (fear)? This debate has not been resolved in the scientific world. The fact is, a thought and an emotion both arise more or less simultaneously, as a response to a trigger.

What ensues is what I call your "story." Your story describes your opinion about what just transpired. It belongs to you. Your story is your view of the situation.

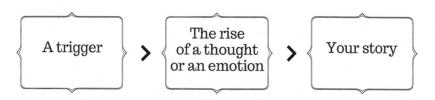

How You Write Your Story: It feels instantaneous, but learning to break down how you get from trigger to story is the first step to getting unstuck.

Sometimes your stories enter and leave your mind smoothly and effortlessly, just as the breath enters and leaves the body. Going back to the example with the snake, once you realize the snake is actually a rope, the story leaves your mind. You move on with your day. You may not even think about that situation ever again.

Yet other times, your story consumes you. When you are stuck on something, your story is all-encompassing. You grasp onto your story and carry it with you for the rest of the day. You keep thinking or talking about your story to yourself or to others. You can't move on from your story. **For our purposes, getting stuck on something is defined as being emotionally attached to one's story**.

This can and does happen to all of us.

We all get stuck on something at one point or another. No one is immune to it. Chances are, if you are wondering at any particular moment if you are stuck on something or not, you could very well be. Yet not everyone is aware when they get stuck on something, and not everyone possesses the tools to get unstuck even when they realize they are stuck. People who get stuck on something and do nothing about it remain stagnant. Not processing through or resolving a situation you are stuck on can lead to internal emotional conflict or conflict with others.

When you get stuck on something, what do you do, if anything? Do you have tools to get unstuck?

The S.T.U.C.K. Method is one such tool. The five-step process: **STOP, TELL, UNCOVER, CONSIDER,** and **O.K.** helps you to get unstuck.

The S.T.U.C.K. Method: Just five steps—easy to remember and use.

The S.T.U.C.K. Method can be processed in one's mind, though I highly recommend writing your thoughts down on paper or on a computer/tablet. Even if your stuck situation is not complicated and does not include a lot of details, and even if you think this writing activity may be "silly" or a waste of time, releasing your thoughts out of your mind and onto paper (or a screen) for you to reflect upon is valuable and therapeutic. Looking at your thoughts written out can help you contemplate them in a more objective way, as if they no longer belong to you.

In this chapter, I will share with you one of my "stuck" stories and highlight how I implemented the step-by-step process. Then, I will delve into The S.T.U.C.K. Method in significantly greater detail to illustrate the value of each step, and then provide you with tips to help you begin on your own.

Stuck on: Acknowledge Me!

I spent the entire day cleaning the house and preparing a beautiful *Shabbat* dinner for my husband and four children. I cleaned the bathrooms, washed the floors, and dusted the house. I cooked a special menu in gratitude for my hardworking husband. In addition to new recipes, I decided to make my husband's favorite eggplant dish (his grandmother's most prized recipe and one that I hardly ever make, because it is too time consuming), as well as fresh bread. And when the family gathered together to eat, I was proud of myself for the clean house we were sitting in and the delicious meal we were about to partake in.

After we welcomed in the *Shabbat* with song and prayer, I set the warm bread on the table alongside three different salads, including my husband's favorite eggplant dish, and we began to eat.

Yet, no one commented on the food.

I was surprised, because I was expecting someone to comment on either the bread or one of the salads, at least.

But no one said a word.

No one even mentioned the unusually immaculate state of the house they were sitting in.

Okay, this is strange. But I bet someone will say something once they taste the soup!

But the soup was served, and still no comments were made.

I started to feel disappointed.

More than anything, I wanted my husband to make a comment of gratitude. For the food. That I slaved over!

Not only that, I wanted him to model gratitude for my children!

To teach them that good husbands acknowledge their hardworking wives!

But alas, nothing.

I served the main dish, confident that *someone* would say something about the new salmon recipe I had prepared for the first time in a cast-iron skillet.

But all I got was complete silence.

I mean, there was talking and noise at the table. Everyone was eating, too.

But, no one was talking about *me*!

About my cooking.

About my hard work!

And how I slaved over this meal!

HELLOOOOOOO???

You are all quite aware that, without me, you would not be eating this meal at this moment, right?

In a spotless house, mind you!

So why isn't anyone saying anything?

I was really upset.

I found myself eating from a place of frustration. For me, that often translates as overeating. I kept reaching for more bread even though I wasn't even hungry.

Then I asked my family members one by one, "What does everyone think about the soup?"

Admittedly, it was passive-aggressive, but I was in that kind of mood.

"You like it? Oh, good! I'm so glad!" I responded.

"And how about Grandma's special eggplant recipe? Anyone like that?" I continued.

"Yes? I'm so happy that you are enjoying your meal!" I continued in an obnoxious tone.

Looking around at blank faces, I realized I was stuck.

Midway through dinner, I recognized that being stuck wasn't getting me anywhere.

Without anyone knowing, I **stopped.**

I closed my eyes and took a couple of deep breaths.

Rather than focusing on what my family was doing—or not doing—I focused on myself.

I noticed a certain tightness in my belly.

I **told** myself, "I am stuck on disappointment."

I then **uncovered** my beliefs and checked the accuracy of each of them:

Belief: I **believe** my husband never cares about me.

Is this 100% accurate? No.

Belief: I **believe** my husband never notices how much work I do around the house.

Is this 100% accurate? No.

Belief: I **believe** my husband doesn't realize how I went out of my way for him to find his grandmother's eggplant recipe.

Is this 100% accurate? Yes, most likely.

Belief: I **believe** my husband is always insensitive and ungrateful.

Is this 100% accurate? No.

Belief: **I believe** good husbands acknowledge their wives all the time.

Is this 100% accurate? No.

When I realized many of my beliefs were unfounded, I came up with a list of possible considerations and other viewpoints to my story.

I can **consider** that I often make dinner and my husband often makes dinner without either of us verbally acknowledging each other.

I can **consider** that I didn't acknowledge my husband today for his work and for being a dependable husband and father.

I can **consider** that my husband had no clue that I was even seeking acknowledgement tonight. He cannot read my mind, and I can't expect him to.

I chose to **consider** that my husband and I often make dinner without either of us verbally acknowledging one another. With that, I verbally acknowledged my husband for the work he did that day and silently acknowledged myself for mine.

I held myself in compassion for getting stuck on disappointment.

It's **O.K.**

STOP

TELL

UNCOVER

CONSIDER

O.K.

S – STOP

All of us have stories running in our minds throughout the day. When you are stuck on something, you know the plot of the story—you are certain of it! You know all the characters. You know their motives and even predict their behaviors. But really, when you are stuck on something, you are only reaffirming your own beliefs to yourself and reinforcing your own point of view. Above all, you know *you* are right, and everyone else around you is *wrong*.

When you initially get stuck on something, you might be unaware that you are stuck, and therefore may not make any conscious efforts to get unstuck. When you do recognize that you are stuck on something, the first step is to **stop.** By stopping, I mean redirecting your attention away from your story to something else real and tangible and attending to that thing fully.

A stop may be internal or external. Here is a list of some of the internal stops I incorporate in my life. I usually combine one or more of them during an active stop. You may prefer to incorporate other stops in your life.

- Close my eyes and take a breath
- Belt out, "Stop!" (Yes, out loud.)
- Clap my hands three times
- Defer a conversation
- Clap my hands three times
- Mindfully listen
- Take a shower
- Pause from responding
- Walk away from the scene
- Count to 10
- Lie down on my yoga mat
- Take 10 deep breaths
- Write in or read from my journal
- Bring my full attention to a new activity, such as: yoga, listening to relaxation music, smelling a flower, staring at a candle, or saying a prayer

Ways I Stop: What Stops Can You Add To This List?

When you are stuck on something, an external stop might also arise unexpectedly. This type of stop is one that awakens you from the story you are in. It is often just as valuable as an internal stop, because it shifts your attention away from your story and prompts you to begin processing The S.T.U.C.K. Method.

Examples of external stops are:

- A loud noise
- Your trigger (a person, typically) leaving the scene
- A sudden resolution to your story
- A memory (such as a previous "stuck" moment)

Enjoy the Stop—It's Good for You

Stopping is an opportunity. It separates you from your story and begins the process that will ultimately guide you to a place of emotional well-being. When we are rushing through life, we often miss the opportunities to stop. But when you do stop, you temporarily put your story on hold and practice being mindful in that moment. You slow down the lightning-fast reactivity and refrain from escalating the situation. When you stop in any one way or combination of ways, you submit to yourself that you are in control and have the ability to break away from the story in order to be present. By stopping, even if momentarily, you also acknowledge that you are preparing to open yourself to alternative ways of perceiving your current situation.

Building Up the Stop Muscle

I should note that though this step, and all the steps of The S.T.U.C.K. Method, are simple in theory, they may not always be easy to implement, especially when you are in the heat of the moment. It's worthwhile, in fact, to practice stopping on a regular basis, even when you are not stuck on something in order to build up your "stop muscle". This cognitive process is akin to learning a new skill or introducing a new habit into your life. It takes lots and lots of practice. There will be many times when you forget or feel unable to stop. But, over time and practice, stopping becomes more familiar and accessible.

The value of the stop is that it enables us to begin the process of stepping outside our stories. In fact, I find the more I stop, the more the practice of stopping engenders more intended (and unintended) useful stops in my life. I practice my stops first thing in the morning, before anyone else in my house wakes up. While most people get up and *go*, I get up and *stop*—on purpose. I find a seat. I focus on my breath and practice not following any thoughts as they arise. When a thought does arise and I become aware my attention is no longer on my breath, I nonjudgmentally acknowledge to where my attention strayed and then return my attention to noticing my breath again. By "noticing my breath," I do not mean I ponder about or evaluate how I am breathing, but rather just notice that I *am* breathing.

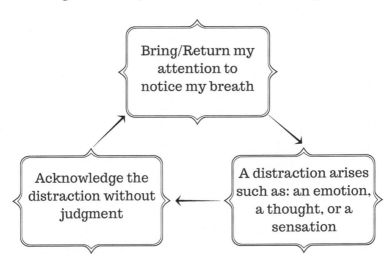

How I Practice Stopping: Most mornings, I take a few minutes to go through this process—no special equipment required.

It is important to note that the stopping practice does not always come easy to me. Sometimes when I sit, I get totally lost in thought and only 20 minutes later recognize I didn't attend to my breath for more than a second. Some days I am more focused than others. This is normal and acceptable and not meant to be judged. The purpose of stopping is the practice itself. Each time I make the time and effort to stop, I benefit, because I offer myself another opportunity to familiarize my mind with the experience of stopping.

The Health Benefits of Stopping

When most people think of ways to improve their physical and mental health, they think of more actions they need to do. But stopping—not doing something—can be just as helpful.

Being stuck on something is a stressor. It is like being in a short-term emergency. When you are stuck on something, your body focuses on survival. Being stuck on something causes your body to react just as it would in a real life-threatening situation, with what is known as our "fight-or-flight" mechanism.

Whether you face a physical stressor (such as defending yourself from a hungry bear) or an emotional stressor (such as defending yourself from someone screaming at you), your body prepares itself physiologically for the situation. Stored energy inside your body quickly rushes outwards to your muscles, stress hormones are released into the bloodstream, heart rate and blood pressure rise, and blood is shunted away from the digestive system. Your body increases strength and speed as if the stressor was a matter of life and death. Your rational mind is also affected during stressful situations; considering the long-term consequences of your behavior is not an option in those moments.

For many of us, getting stuck on something can happen regularly, and getting out of it may not happen as quickly as it does in nature. Some of us are living from one "stuck" moment to another, with no relief in sight. Research shows that there is a harmful effect on our bodies when we face cumulative emotional stressors, one that may lead to a variety of physical or mental illnesses such as heart disease, diabetes, and depression.

I view all of the various stoppings I implement in my life as wellness tools I can draw upon when needed in real-life "emergencies." There are endless opportunities to implement "stops" in your life because *life itself can be your practice*. Your alarm didn't go off in the morning? Someone used up all the hot water before your shower? There's no milk left in the fridge for your morning coffee? There's unexpected traffic on the way to work? Consider the triggers that exist in your life and how instead of viewing them as obstacles, you may view them as your practice. All of the things that typically trigger you in your life are opportunities for you to practice a stop.

You can discover the benefits for yourself with this simple test. The next time you stop, take note of physical sensations in your body. Because the mind and body are intimately connected, when we are stuck on something, we often "hold" our emotions somewhere in the body. Common places people hold their emotions are in their shoulders, backs, stomachs, jaws, and between their eyebrows. The next time you are angry or sad, try to feel where you hold your emotions in your body. Stay with that observation and physical sensation for a moment rather than denying, lashing out at, or withdrawing from it.

There is no need to rush through to the next step of The S.T.U.C.K. Method. You can continue "stopping" and being present with your body for as long as you need or are able. Notice how stopping may affect your physical and mental state by bringing you to a place of momentary calm. Notice how you may feel a physical relief in an area of your body, simply by paying attention to it. The story might still be there with you, but the body begins to release a little.

By redirecting your attention away from your story and toward a stop, you will cause a physiological change that supports the healing process (especially if you also consciously incorporate mindful breathing). The stop can benefit you by slowing your heart rate, and lowering your blood pressure and production of stress hormones. It can help to elicit a relaxation response in your muscles. Stopping is powerful.

You Can Stop Right Here and Now

Consider the value of noticing your breath as an example of a stop. Try it now. When you finish reading this sentence, take a moment to close your eyes, slowly take a deep inhalation and then follow the exhalation until it dissipates. Even if you are not necessarily stuck on something in this very moment, how did paying attention to one complete breath affect you? Consider how taking a mindful breath (or two or three) when you *are* stuck on something might be even more powerful. When you stop amidst a stuck moment, it brings you one step closer to emotional well-being.

Sometimes it is helpful to temporarily pause your active processing through The S.T.U.C.K. Method at "Stop." In other words, you may stop, and then step away from the situation before continuing to process. This doesn't mean you won't continue where you left off. But you can use time to aid in the healing process. I did that during the Shabbat dinner I prepared for my family.

T – TELL

We all have emotions. Lots of them. It is a natural and inevitable part of human life. Even if we try to suppress our emotions, emotion still exist. Acknowledging our emotions is an essential part of The S.T.U.C.K. Method, because it is our attachment to our feelings (and our thoughts) that causes us to feel stuck on something in the first place.

The **tell** step offers you the opportunity to access your emotions. Identify which emotion you are attached to. You may be feeling more than one emotion. Anger and fear can both be present when we feel another person has hurt us. Sadness and longing can coexist as a result of a disappointment or betrayal. If this is the case, you may want to process through The S.T.U.C.K. Method for each of your emotions or process through the most prominent emotion you are feeling in that moment.

Naming the emotion may be challenging. Take your time. Be curious. Try out a few words and see what fits you in that very moment and be sure to watch for self-criticism.

Do you feel fear? Anger? Sadness? Pride? Desire? Check out The S.T.U.C.K. Method's Chart of Emotions to assist you if needed.

Major emotion	Related emotions
Fear	anxiety, apprehension, despair, distress, doubt, embarrassment, fright, horror, insecurity, mortification, nervousness, panic, shock, terror, uncertainty, worry
Anger	aggravation, aggressiveness, agitation, bitterness, defiance, fury, hatred, hostility, lividness, rage, rebellion, spite, vengeance

Aversion	annoyance, apathy, boredom, complacency, contempt, disgust, dislike, displeasure, irritation, resentment, resistance, revulsion, uneasiness
Pride	arrogance, assurance, astonishment, certainty, conceit, confidence, critique, holier than thou, hypocrisy, judgment, opinionated, presumption, rigidity, self-righteousness, surprise, stubbornness, superiority, vain
Gloom	agony, alienation, anguish, despair, defeat, demoralization, depletion, devastation, disappointment, discouragement, disenchantment, distraught, exhaustion, grief, guilt, heartbroken, hopelessness, hurt, inadequacy, isolation, loneliness, longing, loss, neglect, overwhelm, pity, powerlessness, regret, sadness, shame, sorrow, suffering, worthless
Desire	compulsivity, dissatisfaction, envy, frustration, greed, impatience, impulsivity, jealousy, possessiveness, selfishness
Joy	acceptance, anticipation, enthusiasm, excitement, generosity, love, openness

The S.T.U.C.K. Method's Chart of Emotions: At the **tell** step, you'll need to identify your emotion(s). This chart may help. What words resonate for you in this moment?

Allow yourself to feel your emotion. Can you feel it in your body now? Scan your body and identify the spot where you feel it. Where do you feel it? In your belly? In your neck? What does it feel like? Tightness? Achy? Burning? A tight jaw or shoulders? Heart racing? What does it bring about? Nausea? Headache? Allow yourself to notice that feeling—or those feelings.

Detect which emotion you are feeling (or feeling most strongly) and declare it in this clear and precise way: **"I am stuck on ____."**

Notice that when you phrase your emotion as "I am stuck on 'x'" as opposed to "I *am* 'x'" you are separating yourself from the emotion. While in casual conversation you may say, "I am disappointed," by telling yourself "I am *stuck on* disappointment" instead, you give your brain a critical message that while you may be holding on to a certain emotion, that emotion is not your identity. It is merely what you are stuck on, right now, in this moment. Framing your emotion in this way, you will help yourself disentangle from it because you acknowledge that you are independent of it. By affirming your independence, you can begin to understand that whatever emotion you are holding onto is temporary. And as you can get stuck on an emotion, just like you can get stuck on a patch of Velcro, you can also get unstuck from it.

By telling myself that "I am stuck on disappointment" (because my family didn't acknowledge the special dinner I'd made), rather than "I am disappointed," I opened the door to separate myself from this emotion and get unstuck from it.

U – UNCOVER

With this step, we move from our emotions to our thoughts and begin to access the mind. **Uncover** your beliefs about the current situation. Take a moment, close your eyes and imagine yourself back when you were first triggered. What was the first thought or thoughts that came to your mind? Those are examples of your *beliefs.*

Your beliefs may be thoughts about yourself or the world you formulated as an adult, but they also may be thoughts you learned or absorbed from your own childhood, such as: "My mother never listens to me" or "My boss is out to get me" or "I can never do anything right." Dig them all up. Gather as many beliefs that you possibly can about the particular situation and write them down.

Just as in the **tell** step, here, too, there is a recommended way to articulate your beliefs. Begin each belief statement with "**I believe…**" as opposed to simply naming them one by one. As you state each belief (or after you compile your full list), reflect upon each one. Check each one's validity. Ask yourself, "Is this 100% accurate?"

Keep in mind that most of our beliefs are not entirely accurate. Often, our beliefs are exaggerations, generalizations, or categorizations. One clue to this is when belief statements include words such as:

Absolutely	Constantly	Never
All	Definitely	Should
Always	Entirely	Should not
Certain	Needs to	Sure
Completely	Most	Totally

Common Words Used in Belief Statements: Staying aware of the usage of these words in your belief statements may help you determine the accuracy of a belief.

By beginning each belief statement with, "**I believe** ..." each time, you will remind yourself, whether you can see it in that moment or not, that your beliefs are just *beliefs,* not certainties. By declaring, "**I believe**...," you are affirming that your beliefs are not facts, and therefore they can be questioned and examined, and, when appropriate, released. Notice if any of your beliefs do not entirely hold true. Be honest with yourself. You may uncover feelings of shame or embarrassment with some of the things that come to mind. Don't worry. Your beliefs do not reflect who you are as a whole, but rather serve to support your feelings in that current moment.

That being said, it is important to recognize what you believe. Your story is likely to be slanted in ways that support your beliefs, and therefore you will behave in ways consistent with them. By now, you're probably recognizing that some of your beliefs can be obstacles. Whether they are true or not, our beliefs function as a protection mechanism. These beliefs may temporarily help us. They typically are self-congratulatory and make us feel morally superior. They serve us ... until they don't. It is our work to realize when our beliefs are serving us (i.e., when they motivate us and propel us toward actions that truly benefit us or others), and when challenging our beliefs might allow us to uncover a deeper, more beneficial, universal truth.

Keep in mind it may be easy to confuse thoughts with emotions, as these regularly influence one another. For example, "I believe I am really disappointed because my husband is not acknowledging me!" is an emotion and should be listed under **Tell** rather than **Uncover.**

C – CONSIDER

The moment you notice that one or more of your beliefs is not 100% accurate is the moment you begin to realize the foundation of your story may be weak and even baseless. That is, we recognize that the story we had in mind is exactly that, a story; one based on a narrow perspective rooted in current emotions and fixed ways of thinking.

By considering other perspectives to the story, we acknowledge that being stuck on an emotion limits our view, and we deliberately seek other viewpoints so we can see better. Practice stretching your "considering muscles" is similar to creating new neural pathways. Expand your mind's capacity to think more broadly to include all imaginable angles and perspectives for this particular situation.

When taking on new considerations, you shift from emotional responses to rational thinking. At this point, you may not actually accept all of these considerations. That is fine. All you need to do is acknowledge them as possibilities. Start a list offering new perspectives to your story. I've found the most useful way to articulate considerations is through sentences beginning with "**I can consider that**…"

Sometimes, in the heat of the moment, it is difficult to internally generate considerations. For that reason, I keep a number of considerations as go-to examples when I find it difficult to access ones specific to the situation. (See page 42.)

Choose at least one new perspective from your list to "take on." You, and only you, can make this choice. If you find you cannot possibly take on anything new, ponder whether you may be stuck on something deeper than the emotion you have already named. You may need to process The S.T.U.C.K. Method with an additional emotion or even with a previous stuck story that has yet to be resolved.

The emotion you were attached to may linger. You can't necessarily control it and push it out of your life. But you can cradle it in a different way of thinking.

I can consider that:
• The person deserves the benefit of the doubt.
• The person probably had good intentions.
• I do not know the whole story.
• The other person is stuck and may deserve my compassion.
• I can be grateful for ...
• I can let this situation go and learn from this experience for the future.
• This situation is unusual, and rather than be stuck on it I am free to say, "oh well," "no big deal," "this is also for the good," or "this too shall pass."

Go-to Consideration Examples: What other considerations can you add?

WARNING - Extremely Important to Consider:
If you believe your life or health is in imminent danger with the "stuck" situation you are in, do not consider other perspectives. Get immediate help.

K - O.K.

There may be a moment, when processing through The S.T.U.C.K. Method, you feel guilt, shame, or embarrassment for getting stuck on something in the first place. This step reminds you to be compassionate towards yourself.

We all get stuck on something. And it's O.K. If we do not hold ourselves in compassion when we get stuck, we'd be beating ourselves up every day. Accept your human imperfections and forgive yourself.

Remind yourself what you told yourself in the second step (T, for **tell**) and affirm the following: "I got stuck on ___ and it's **O.K.**"

This final step closes the process of The S.T.U.C.K. Method. This doesn't necessarily mean that your emotion has entirely subsided. It may indeed linger. Yet, by ceremoniously closing the process, you offer yourself the opportunity to move on to emotional well-being, without allowing your emotions to fester.

When I get stuck on something, I hope to recognize and attend to it sooner each time. The more I process using The S.T.U.C.K. Method, the more I find myself flowing through life with a greater sense of emotional well-being.

We all get stuck.	I'm fine.	I'm all right.
I am O.K.	Things happen.	It'll be O.K.
I forgive myself.	I'm human.	I did my best.

Words of Self-Compassion: Be kind to yourself.

Part II: Emotions We Get Stuck On

When I first wrote down the steps of The S.T.U.C.K. Method, I had already been practicing it informally for a while. I would use it to get through obstacles small and large. Seeing the reflections of my thoughts on paper or a computer screen revealed the workings of my mind. As I jotted down my stories, I noticed certain patterns occurring. I realized I always expressed my emotions from one perspective: my biased perspective. And that often, I got stuck in that perspective.

Each time I reflected on my singular perspective, however, I gained mental clarity into my narrow view. I was able to make this connection: the emotions I experienced came from within me. With clearer insight, I recognized that the only real way to get unstuck was to be truly present, identify my emotions, acknowledge that the beliefs I hold are not always accurate, consider that other ways of perceiving exist, and hold myself in self-compassion for when I get stuck in the first place. As soon as I began to do this, I found my mind opening up to new ways of thinking and understanding.

The practice of noticing, of being mindful, is a big thing. But being aware I was stuck was not enough for me. I wanted to get unstuck. Or at least to try to prevent unpleasant, unproductive situations from recurring. For me, as for many of us, the most difficult behavior patterns are repetitive. We keep getting stuck on the same stuff, time and time again. I needed a supportive tool to help me get unstuck. While practices like yoga and even meditation helped me be cognizant of my thoughts, I didn't find within these practices the guidance I needed to get unstuck.

It was out of this desire for an active next step that I created The S.T.U.C.K. Method. As I talked it over with friends, I began to see and hear that The S.T.U.C.K. Method would be worth sharing—that it could help people. At first, I kept a journal recording my "stuck" stories. When I began blogging about them, I never anticipated having a large audience. But when I started to share my stories, I discovered quite by accident that sharing my stories inspired others. I have learned that what is most personal is often times most universal. I received comments and email from people sharing their own stories and how The S.T.U.C.K. Method helped them. From this, I learned that nothing makes a stronger impression than a personal story.

In all of my stories, the first thing I notice is my emotion. My emotions are big and they are real. Noticing that I am stuck on an emotion is what signals me to stop. From my stories, I was able to identify seven major emotions that appear regularly in my life: fear, anger, aversion, pride, gloom, desire, and joy as well as other emotions that I categorize within each of these primary ones.

For this section, I've gathered stories from my blog that received lots of reaction, and some new stories. Each story relates to one of these seven major emotions identified in the chart. You may choose to read this section chapter by chapter or if any one of the major emotions is one you tend to get stuck on often, you may choose to focus on that chapter first. Following each chapter appears a workbook page. When you finish reading each chapter, consider stopping and reflecting on a "stuck" story you may be currently in or have experienced recently. These workbook pages exist for your benefit. They are an opportunity to practice and I strongly urge you to try them out.

Chapter name	Emotions found in this section
Fear	anxiety, despair, embarrassment, fear, insecurity, panic, worry
Anger	agitation, anger, rage
Aversion	annoyance, aversion, uneasiness

Pride	holier than thou, judgment, self-righteousness, rigidity
Gloom	anguish, despair, disappointment, gloom, guilt, powerlessness, regret, shame
Desire	desire, frustration, jealousy
Joy	anticipation, excitement, generosity

Find Your Emotion: Here's a key to quickly finding stories about particular emotions you may get stuck on.

While many of the stories in this chapter incorporate the exact words of The S.T.U.C.K. Method process, others incorporate similar words or phrases to illustrate the process. Either way, the steps or the key phrases relating to the steps are in bold, to help you follow the process.

My hope is that my stories will inspire you to consider trying The S.T.U.C.K. Method for yourself and recognize how it can be a guiding light in your life, just as it is in mine.

Chapter 1: FEAR

Stuck on: Potato Chips Will Make Me Fat!

I went food shopping the other day.

I meant to arrive at the supermarket around 4:30 p.m., to be home in enough time to prepare dinner.

But I made some other stops along the way and was delayed.

As I walked into the market, around 6 p.m., I started to hear my stomach growl.

Uh-oh.

I'm hungry.

But I have no food with me.

And yet I was standing inside a supermarket, surrounded by food.

If there's one thing I don't handle well, it's being hungry.

If there's another thing I don't handle well, it's being hungry while inside a supermarket.

Quick, finish your shopping, and go home to prepare dinner!

But I knew a quick shop on a Thursday evening in Israel wasn't going to happen. Too crowded.

What can I buy that's somewhat healthy?

An apple?

No. I have no place to wash that.

Same thing for the veggies.

I felt my stomach rumble again.

So, I went over to the cheese counter and asked to sample a piece of hard cheese.

That was a good idea, Shira.

That'll hold you over until you get home.

I ate it.

I enjoyed it.

I thought it would hold me over.

But it didn't.

Rumble, rumble.

Now what?

As I contemplated how to satisfy my belly, I turned to see the next person in line at the cheese counter, holding an open bag of potato chips. Not just any potato chips. Beet-and sweet-potato chips.

I started salivating.

I want those!

And I knew the most direct route to get them.

I made a beeline over to the potato chip aisle.

Wait, Shira, you don't want to eat those potato chips!

You don't eat processed food!

Potato chips will make you fat!

Find a healthier choice.

Go for the rice crackers!

So, I took a detour over to the rice crackers.

Yuck!

Rice crackers?

B-O-R-I-N-G!

Go for the potato chips!

Didn't you see? They're healthy!

They're made from real whole vegetables!

Much better than eating puffed rice!

And you're hungry for crying out loud!

What's the big deal?

And there I was.

Standing in the supermarket.

In a duel with myself.

What am I afraid of?

I'm just hungry, for crying out loud!

I **stopped in my tracks** and closed my eyes.

I took a deep breath and noticed the physical sensations of an empty belly.

I was **stuck on fear**.

I heard a little voice that was telling me that **potato chips will make me fat**.

And another voice questioning that **belief**.

I **considered** what eating a bag of potato chips will do to me in that moment.

Would it satisfy my hunger?

Yes.

Would it make me fat?

No.

So, I walked back to the potato chips aisle.

I picked the bag off the shelf, opened it, and mindfully tasted the first beet chip that I've had in years.

Mmmmmmmmm.

I delighted in the moment.

It felt emotionally and physically satisfying.

I got stuck on fear of gaining weight.

I'm sure I'm not the first.

I'm glad I was able to process through it and honor my body, which was signaling that it needed fuel.

I came to recognize that it's fine to eat beet-and sweet-potato chips when I'm hungry in the supermarket.

In fact, it's more than fine.

It's divine.

Stuck on: Frozen in Fear

Not long ago, a war took place in Israel.

And as most wars do, it shook me up a bit.

But because the war took place in the south, and I live in the north, I wasn't as on edge as other residents in this country, whose homes and communities were constantly being bombarded by missiles.

While staying abreast of the news, I also tried to live my life as normally as possible.

That wasn't easy, especially with half of the men in our community absent, having been called up to the reserves.

In an attempt to do something normal, I decided to attend the men's basketball game that was scheduled to take place one night in my community.

A few days earlier, my husband got a phone call from one of the guys who plays in the local basketball league asking if he'd be willing to sub, because too many of the men on the team weren't around.

I was eager to watch my husband play in the game. Yet when I walked up to the court, five minutes into the beginning of the game, I froze in fear.

Because all I heard was yelling.

In Arabic.

I stood panic-stricken for a few moments.

What's going on?

Are there terrorists here?

Should I run home?

Break to the nearest safe room?

But, it didn't take me long to realize what was going on.

The Arabic was coming from the opposing team, a neighboring Muslim community in our municipality.

And, the yelling wasn't anything you may be hearing out of the words of Hamas terrorists, such as:

"Kill the Jews!" or

"Destroy Israel!" or

"Jews back to Auschwitz. Hitler was right!"

Instead, the yelling was the typical yelling you'd hear on a basketball court.

"Hey, ref! That was a foul! Are you blind?"

"Double dribble!"

"Back court!"

"Rebound! Come on! Rebound!"

"*Nu*, ref? Can't you count? How long you gonna let him stay in the key?"

The realization of what was truly happening **stopped** me in my tracks.

I noticed I was holding my breath.

I was so **stuck on fear** that, in the moment, I **believed** Arabic language equals terrorism, and that Arabic has no place on the basketball court in my own community.

I was too frozen in fear to realize my beliefs were flawed.

And I forgot to **consider** that Israel has reached a place where Jewish and Muslim men can come together and play basketball in peace.

I released a long exhalation and smiled to myself.

I got stuck on fear, but it's **O.K.**

I chose to witness the beautiful scene.

Two communities.

Two religions.

Playing basketball in peace.

Giving each other high-fives at the end of the game and walking off the court together.

Going home peacefully.

Just like any other day.

Stuck on: Where's My Shopping Cart?

Six years ago, my family moved from New Jersey to a small *kibbutz* in Northern Israel.

I love our community here.

One thing I love most is the shared family *Shabbat* meals.

One Friday morning, I invited a family for dinner for that same night.

It was a last-minute invitation and I forgot to check how much food we had in the house.

Upon checking, I felt we didn't have enough food and realized I needed to go food shopping.

And while I loathe food shopping on Friday mornings in Israel, because of the stress everyone is in rushing around before the stores close for *Shabbat*, I didn't really have a choice if I wanted to prepare a festive dinner.

So I took the car to the nearest supermarket to do a quick shop and was quite proud to be finished shopping in less than 20 minutes.

As I stood on line at the cashier, I looked down into my cart and noticed that there were things in it I didn't recognize.

Strange! I thought to myself. *Perhaps someone accidentally put one or two items into my cart?*

I started to remove those items and place them on a random shelf.

But then I realized that nothing at all seemed right about this cart.

It was not my cart!

It was someone else's!

Agh!

Somebody took my cart!

Oh, man!

Why me?

Who has time for this?

It's Friday and I need to get home and start cooking!

I don't have time to start shopping all over again!

I was stuck on panic.

I started to push the cart around the supermarket in hopes of finding the culprit. And in doing so, I lost my breath, as it is not so easy to run around a supermarket while pushing a loaded cart.

Suddenly, I realized it would be easier to park the anonymous cart and continue to look for my own cart without the additional load.

I approached every shopper in the market, eyed the contents of their baskets and asked, "Are you sure this cart is yours?"

I got lots of strange looks.

Which made me angry.

Why are shoppers so mindless?

Why are people always in such a rush?

Why can't things ever be easy?

I just need to get home!

With food for dinner!

And then it dawned on me that I had an even bigger problem than my frustration—at the bottom of my missing cart lay my cell phone and the keys to my car.

(Yes, placing my phone and keys at the bottom of my cart is a bad, bad habit, and I don't do that anymore!)

I ran to the customer service desk.

I was out of breath at that point.

"My cart!"

"Someone has it!"

"And my car keys!"

"And my phone!"

"They're all in the cart!" I cried.

My yelling and panting got everyone moving.

Security men started to check the recent footage from the

hidden cameras.

One supermarket employee called my cell phone, but no one answered.

Another did a sweep similar to the one I did, but came up with nothing.

I ran to the parking lot to see if my car was still there.

It was.

Thank God.

I began to head back inside, but reconsidered.

Should I guard my car in case the ~~shopper~~ bandit plans on stealing it, too?

I chose to go back inside.

But, I continued to run around making a spectacle of myself in search of my missing cart.

Yelling.

Cursing.

Crying about how this was going to ruin my day!

And that no one was helping me!

How I was all alone in this world!

I couldn't think straight.

I felt my heart beating a million times a second.

And of course, in all my upset, I couldn't even recognize another perspective existed:

Perhaps *nobody* took my cart in the first place.

But rather *I* took someone *else's* cart!

And that *my cart* is still standing where I left it.

And that perhaps it was *I* who was the mindless one, not some random Israeli I'd been accusing for the past 20 minutes.

And, you know what?

When a supermarket employee asked if that unoccupied cart near the dairy counter was mine, I hesitated to check.

Because I knew the answer.

I knew it was mine.

And yet, when my cart finally showed up, I stumbled upon, too, a "natural" **stop**.

I returned the cart I accidentally "stole" and profusely apologized to the man who came to claim it.

I realized that, when **stuck on panic, I believed** everyone else around me was mindless, without speculating whether that belief was justifiable or not.

And therefore, I did not **consider** the possibility it was I who was the mindless one in the story.

I also **acknowledged** how being stuck not only created personal anxiety, but havoc for so many other people in the supermarket.

I got stuck on many emotions that day while frantically looking for my cart, but it's **O.K.**

What I wanted most was to bring in *Shabbat* with happiness and joy.

Which is exactly what I did.

Stuck on: I Need My Nurse!

Four days into one of our annual family vacations, I landed in the hospital with spontaneous peritonitis.

I tried to put off emergency surgery, but when I went into septic shock, there was no choice but to have two back-to-back abdominal surgeries.

When I woke up from the anesthesia 24 hours later, I learned I was intubated and therefore could not speak.

I was scared and confused.

The many intensive care nurses that came and left administered pain medications, took my vitals, and attended to me when I rang for them.

But scared to death and without the ability to speak, I really needed something more than a nurse.

I needed an angel.

But I had a team of rotating nurses. And often, I felt like a burden to them and this often left me feeling hurt and angry.

Like when one nurse walked into my room, after having rung for her, and asked, "Yes?"

Yes?

I've got a BREATHING tube down my throat!

I.CAN'T. SPEAK!

But I tried not to get stuck on anger.

And, thank God, it wasn't always like that.

Because I actually was blessed with an angel.

One nurse assigned to my room turned out to be the antithesis of all the other nurses I met up until that point. She was my angel.

She was caring, funny, experienced, and compassionate.

"How can I help?" she would ask, before I even rang for her.

"It looks to me that you're sitting kind of funny. Can I move some pillows around for you?" she'd say.

Plus, she had a great sense of humor, which I really needed during that time.

(Like her conspiracy theories that my father and husband were FBI agents, each having their own swipe cards leading up to the back entrance of the hospital, allowing them to enter on their own time and bypass security.)

I wasn't afraid to bother this angel.

Just the opposite.

She encouraged me to express anything I wanted and she calmed me when I felt anxious.

Like when she found a spot of blood on the pillow underneath my knees.

I freaked.

She didn't.

"Do you have your period?" she asked.

"No!" I scribbled furiously.

"CALL. THE. DOCTOR!!!" I chicken scratched on my pad as fast as I could.

"Wait a minute," she said calmly. "Let's see if we can make sense of this."

And, she did.

It was the heparin shot in my leg that had slightly bled into the pillow.

When Angela was in my room, I felt safe and supported, happy and protected.

But the next morning I woke up to the sight of another nurse.

I wrote on my clipboard, "Where's Angela?"

"Oh, she's not on duty now. I'm your nurse today."

What?

No!

I flipped out.

How could Angela leave me?

I'm not healed yet!

I need her!

No one else knows how to take care of me like Angela does!

I knew it was going to be a bad day.

I knew the nurses would be less than sympathetic to me.

I knew they would lose patience with the fact that I couldn't use my voice.

And that I'd only be happy if Angela were there.

But I caught myself when my aunt walked into the room for a visit.

Seeing her face and knowing she was going to spend a good part of the day with me helped me feel some relief and prompted me to **stop**.

I closed my eyes and **told** myself I was stuck on panic.

I **uncovered** my belief about needing Angela, and Angela only, as my nurse.

But upon reflection, I realized that belief was unsubstantiated.

I **considered** that the day didn't necessarily have to go downhill just because Angela wasn't taking care of me.

And that I'd most likely make it through the day just fine.

I got stuck on panic, but I was **O.K.**

So, when a male nurse came into my room that morning, gave me my meds and asked, "How are you feeling today? On a scale of one to 10, what's your pain level? Can I help you with anything?"

I smiled and shook my head.

Because I was fine.

Stuck on: Am I Going to Die?

My prognosis was inconclusive.

The doctors could not figure out the source of the infection.

Would it come back?

Why did this happen?

Should we expect something more serious to happen at a later date?

And while the doctors may have felt confident that the worst was behind me, I wasn't.

What if this is the end of my life?

What if I'm going to die in this hospital room?

What about my kids?

My husband?

I whimpered while lying awake and alone in the cold,

hospital room.

I was very, very stuck on anxiety.

And then a visitor came.

A rabbi friend.

He said something to me that struck me more than any other visitor's words of comfort or prayer and caused me to **stop**.

"Speak to God," he suggested.

He must have seen confusion on my face, because he repeated it.

"Really. Just speak to God. Like you're having a conversation. Tell God your fears. Ask of God. But above all, just speak to God."

Talk to God?

In the ICU?

Are you kidding?

What should I say?

Do I speak out loud, or just in my heart?

And how much time should I take from God's precious time?

Yikes! Talking to God is something I've never done before.

But I considered it might not be such a bad idea.

So I did.

I whispered to God in as loud a whisper as possible so God would hear me, but the nurses wouldn't.

(I didn't want anyone thinking that the painkillers were affecting my sanity.)

"I'm feeling anxious."

"I **need to** know, has my time come?" I asked through tears.

"I need more time on this earth! I'm not ready to die!"

"I need to know! Answer me!"

But as I reflected on my statements, I realized I didn't really need to know the answer to those questions.

In fact, I realized that no one has the answers to those questions.

I **considered** how everyone—the doctors, the nurses, and my family—were keeping me abreast of my status and prognosis, even though the cause of the infection was still unknown.

And I considered I had little reason to feel anxious, as there was a whole host of people looking out for me.

I got stuck on anxiety, but that's **O.K.**

The suggestion to talk to God brought me to the present moment and helped me get unstuck.

Stuck on: Were They in a Terrorist Attack?

One night last winter, my husband and daughter, along with a few others from our community, traveled in two cars to go see the play, "The Wave."

The show is based on an extraordinary novel that tells a true-life story from the 1960s, of a California high school that began an experiment exploring the nature of fascism, which rapidly ran out of control.

I saw the movie version when I was in high school.

It had made an indelible impression on me, and that was why I wanted my 12-year-old daughter to see the play as well.

Especially because she started reading Holocaust literature on her own this year.

So she went with this group from our community, and apparently, the play was amazing.

Yet I didn't hear that from her.

My husband told me.

When he arrived home solo.

"Where's Ayalah?" I asked my husband, as he entered the house with a bag of groceries.

"She's not home yet? I told her I needed to stop at the grocery store after the play, but she didn't want to go with me. She went back with the rest of the group in the other car. She should have been home over an hour ago," he said.

Not the kind of news any parent wants to hear.

Where could they be?

I bet they just stopped for a bite to eat.

So I called my daughter.

But she didn't answer her cell phone.

I called every adult that was supposed to be in that car.

No one answered.

I sent one of them a text message.

No response.

I started to call the spouses.

But they hadn't heard from their family members either.

And then I started to get anxious.

I started to think the worst.

Because that's what you do when you live in the Middle East.

Think the worst.

Because the worst happens here.

I stepped outside so as not to frighten the rest of my family.

I was sure the group was in a terrorist attack.

I was certain of it.

No!

This can't be happening!

I started to imagine the bloody scene.

And how I'd have to come and identify the body.

Tears started rushing down my face.

And ...

And then, I heard footsteps.

Down the path from our house.

But it was dark.

I couldn't see a thing.

"Ayalah?" I called out.

"Yeah, hi *Ema*."

"I called you! You didn't answer!" I yelled at her.

"Yeah, I just got the message now. I didn't have any reception. We stopped for pizza. What's wrong? It looks like you were crying," she replied.

I let out a big sigh of relief.

Pizza?

I chuckled to myself.

That's where you were?

"How was the show?" I stammered out.

"Great! I'm so glad I went!" my daughter replied.

Witnessing my daughter safe and sound and hearing her joy about the evening, prompted me to **stop.**

I **told** her how I got stuck on anxiety when I couldn't locate her or anyone else in the group and how I **was sure** they were in a terrorist attack.

Frozen in fear, I didn't check the accuracy of that belief and realize the unlikelihood of it, nor did I **consider** anything, but the worst.

"It's okay, *Ema*. Everyone's a little on edge these days. Next time, I'll try to be in better touch, so that you don't have to worry."

I got stuck on anxiety and fear.

But, **I forgave myself**.

And then went on to count my blessings.

Stuck on: What if My Daughter Gets Kidnapped?

One night last summer, my husband took our daughter to the airport to fly to the States.

An approximate 11-hour flight.

She would be traveling alone, as she has for the past five years, since we moved to Israel.

My husband and I had decided when she was 8 years old that she was mature enough to make this trip on her own.

Because she's not really on her own.

She's accompanied by an airline escort.

Which is the airline's regulation if the child is under 16 years old.

There is a $100 fee for this service.

Which we don't mind paying because knowing she is under someone's responsibility until she arrives in the hands of my waiting parents, is priceless.

I've always felt at ease with this situation.

Until my husband returned from the airport that night explaining to me that this time there was no escort.

What are you talking about?

No escort?

How could that be?

"Why? What happened?" I asked.

Apparently the airline was doing a trial offer: parents of children 12 and older could opt to hire an escort or not.

I didn't understand.

I mean, I understood this in theory, but I didn't understand how this temporary regulation pertained to us.

"Ayalah still needs an escort, no matter what the airline's

new policy is, right?"

No answer.

"Right?" I asked again, waiting confirmation.

Apparently, my husband disagreed.

Because she's already grown up.

And can fly on her own.

So he chose to send her solo.

"You what?" I screamed.

"You decided that on your own?"

"What about me?"

"Don't I have a say in the matter?"

"Well—" my husband started to say.

"Who's going to help her with her luggage?" I continued.

"What about all the forms she needs to fill out?"

"She'll be fine," he said matter-of-factly.

"What if she can't find my parents?" I cried.

"What if she gets lost?"

I started to cry.

"She won't get lost," he said, losing patience with me.

"I didn't send her with any money," I told him. "She has no cell phone!"

"She won't need either of those," he said calmly.

"I don't want her talking to strangers!" I bawled. "For crying out loud! She's only 12! What if she gets kidnapped? She's my baby!"

"Shira! SHE. WILL. BE. FINE. She's done this before," my husband said, gritting his teeth.

I was so mad at my husband for making this decision alone.

More than that, I was afraid for my daughter's safety!

I **stormed out of the house**.

And let out a scream.

Agh!!!

I counted to 10 as slowly as I could.

I **told** myself I was stuck on anxiety.

I **thought** about how my daughter absolutely wanted an escort, and how she was probably scared to death now.

I also **thought** about how my husband is always so cheap.

A few minutes passed before I recognized my beliefs were probably not entirely true. I was still scared and angry, but somehow able to counter my beliefs with others.

I so wished I could have spoken to her in that moment.

But I couldn't.

She was already in the sky, heading to the United States.

Maybe she'll be fine.

Maybe nothing will happen.

Most likely nothing will happen.

Considering all of this, I walked back into the house.

And asked my husband that next time, we make this kind of decision together.

I told him I got stuck on fear, but **I was fine**. At least, almost fine. I'd feel better once I knew my daughter arrived safely.

I cradled the lingering fear in my knowledge that my daughter has done this flight many times before, (albeit with an escort), she's mature, and the chances that something will go wrong are slim to none.

And I let it go when I went to sleep, as it was really out of my hands at that point anyway.

When I read the email first thing in the morning that she had arrived and was in the arms of my parents, I was relieved.

Which made me consider whether my husband had made the right decision after all.

Stuck on: My Kids Will Be Traumatized!

One night in 2014, I drove my 9-year-old son to the airport for his annual summer visit to New Jersey to spend time with his grandparents.

I noticed my son was attentive during the 1½-hour car ride, looking out the window, and commenting on things he's never seen before.

He was also persistent with questions regarding the war Israel was in the midst of - Operation Protective Edge.

"*Ema*, where's the airport located?"

"Near Tel Aviv," I said.

"Wait a minute. Aren't rockets being shot at Tel Aviv from Gaza?"

"Yes."

"Are we going to be in rocket range?"

"I don't know."

"Can we go another way? Like ... can we avoid the rockets?"

"No. There is no other way to get to the airport."

"*Ema* ... did you see that billboard? It showed what we're supposed to do if you hear a siren."

"No, I missed it," I said, starting to get uncomfortable with his feelings of insecurity.

"It said, 'Pull your car to the side immediately. Get out. Distance yourself from your car. Bend down and cover your and your children's heads. Then listen for further instructions'."

Wow.

Why does my kid need to know such things?

Responding to my silence, he asked, "What? You didn't know that? You don't know what to do in case you hear a siren?"

"No. I mean, yes. I know. I'm just surprised by the billboard."

"*Ema,* did you know that the shrapnel falling from the demolition of the rockets are more dangerous than the rockets themselves?"

"Wait a minute. How do you know that?"

"I heard it from my friends."

"Really? You talked about that with your friends?" I said, dumbfounded.

"Yeah ... of course."

This is what my kids are talking about at school?

When we arrived at the airport, my son asked, "*Ema* ... see that sign? It's pointing to the security room. But where is the room actually? I don't see it. Do you?"

"No. I can't see it from where we're standing."

"Well, should we ask where it is? Just in case?"

"No, I think if a siren starts, we'll hear instructions. Plus, we can just follow the crowd. I bet other people know where it is," I said trying to sound convincing.

How is this war affecting my children?

What are the short-term effects?

The long-term effects?

How is it affecting them emotionally?

Socially?

Spiritually?

Philosophically?

Psychologically?

Consciously?

Unconsciously?

Maybe we shouldn't have moved to Israel.

Living here will damage and traumatize my children!

What terrible parents we are for having moved our family to the Middle East!

What were we thinking?

After passing through security and waiting at the gate with my son for the escort to pick him up, there was a news flash on the television:

"Terror attack in Jerusalem—one pedestrian killed, seven injured, terrorist shot dead."

Did my son see that?

I turned to my son and gave him a huge hug.

Feeling emotional, I squeezed him tight before he boarded on the 747 heading to Philadelphia.

I **mindfully watched him** as he took one step at a time towards the gate.

I noticed I was **stuck on worry and despair** and checked in with the beliefs that arose in my mind.

I knew they weren't 100% accurate.

As I watched my son board, and saw his huge smile of excitement, I also **considered** that these wars, as unfortunate as they are, come in cycles.

Most days, my children lead normal lives, just like kids their age in the United States: They go to school, attend their extracurricular activities, and spend time with family.

And yes, there is war, and there is terrorism.

But to my dismay, war and terrorism are not limited only to Israel.

Maybe living in Israel will actually prepare my children for the real world.

And they will recognize that evil exists.

Instead of pretending it doesn't.

I got stuck on a few emotions, but **I'm fine with it**.

Ignoring the reality doesn't help.

Processing through it allowed me to be aware of emotions— my own and my child's—that I hadn't been previously paying attention to.

Stuck on: I Am So Embarrassed!

I was sitting at a holiday meal recently when our host served the first course.

Chicken soup.

As I sat patiently waiting for the host to serve me, I noticed my husband start on his soup.

I was shocked.

Do you have no manners?

What about eating etiquette?

As my mind raced, I watched him drink the remainder of his soup (yes, he actually brought the bowl up to his mouth and slurped it down to the last drop) even before the host had a chance to sit down.

I was appalled.

I was embarrassed.

I was afraid the host would be insulted.

I felt so averse to sitting at that table with my husband.

Especially as guests in someone else's home!

I wanted to crawl underneath the table and hide.

Now, if it had been my child, I probably would have said

aloud, "Wait for others, please, before starting to eat."

But, it was my *husband*.

What to do?

Parent him?

This approach never works for us.

It is never effective, pleasant, or welcomed.

I bet he's probably doing this just to annoy me!

As emotional as I was in that moment, I didn't want the host to know, and somewhere deep inside, I also didn't want to ruin this nice dinner with friends.

So, I **closed my eyes** for a brief second and took a deep breath and noticed how my fist was grasping my spoon.

I loosened my grip.

I was **stuck on embarrassment**.

Just as I was opening my eyes, the host came to the table, noticed my husband's empty bowl, and chuckled out loud, "Hey, why don't you have some soup, won't you? Actually, I'm glad you finished it while it was hot. Would you like some more?"

WHAT?

Was the host laughing with my husband?

And not at him?

The host wasn't even upset?

My **beliefs** weren't accurate?

In that moment, I **considered** that while my husband and I are a unit, we are also separate. His behavior is not necessarily a reflection of me or my values.

And by starting on his soup before everyone else was served, he wasn't trying to annoy me.

He was just eating the way he always does.

In a free and uninhibited way.

Because that is *his* way.

And not mine.

And that's **O.K.**

I was grateful I was able to process through my embarrassment before causing an unfortunate scene as I've done in the past.

And with that, I picked up my spoon and enjoyed my own soup.

It was extra delicious.

Stuck on: I'm Not Good Enough

Ever since I moved to Israel, I haven't taught much yoga.

When I lived in New Jersey, I taught several classes a week, in yoga studios and health centers, for groups of anywhere from eight to 25 people.

It has been about four years since I've taught a regular yoga class.

And for me, that's like being a fish out of water.

The reason I haven't taught a yoga class in four years is because I didn't have a space conducive to teach classes.

There were no public buildings on the *kibbutz* and my home is too small to accommodate people for a yoga class.

After four years of waiting, a new youth hall was built in my community, which gave me the chance to get back into teaching.

This building contains a large all-purpose room (perfect for teaching a yoga class to up to 20 people) and three small classrooms (for teaching up to six students).

People in the community had previously expressed interest in a yoga class, so it was a no-brainer for me to start one immediately.

I chose a night of the week to teach and advertised it to the community.

On the night of the first class, I arrived early, heated up the large all-purpose room (expecting at least 10 people to show up), set the ambience with candles, put on relaxation music, and waited.

But, only my husband and one other woman showed up.

And that was it for the night.

I managed to not get stuck on disappointment, recognizing it was the middle of the winter and people have a hard time leaving their cozy homes at night.

Nonetheless, teaching to a class of two in a space that can fit 20 made me feel sad.

The space felt empty, my energy lost.

I didn't mention this to the woman or my husband, but I was concerned that neither would return for another class. I was certain they also suffered from the lack of ambience. As a practitioner, I've always found ambience to be a significant factor in whether or not I enjoy a yoga class.

When I dug even deeper, I realized an empty room represented more to me. True or not, an empty room meant I wasn't a good enough teacher to fill it. Or so I thought.

A good yoga teacher would be able to fill up the big room.

And have lots of students.

And I only have a few.

Which means people don't like my classes.

And if people don't like my classes, then what am I doing teaching yoga in the first place?

I may not have been stuck on disappointment, but my worry indicated I was stuck on insecurity. I was worried I wasn't good enough.

I stopped at my front door on my way home and **took a few breaths** before I walked into the house.

And **told** myself I was stuck on insecurity.

I reflected on my **beliefs** and knew they weren't true.

I reminded myself I had a great reputation as a yoga teacher back in New Jersey.

And **considered** I could teach in the small room instead of the all-purpose room. After all, teaching in a small room does not reflect who I am as a teacher.

In fact, teaching in a small room could create a more intimate space, a space where the students would feel more attention from me than they would in a large space where energy can get lost.

And that teaching in a small room could create more physical warmth on these cold nights.

I got stuck on insecurity, but **I'm fine**.

The following week, I welcomed my two students into the small room with a renewed sense of love, presence, and confidence.

Open Workbook Pages – Stuck on Fear

One comment I've received repeatedly as I've shared my stories and The S.T.U.C.K. Method is that people admire my willingness to be vulnerable. I also urge others to take the opportunity to be vulnerable, identify the emotions they feel, and process through them.

Can you think of a time you were stuck on fear, or any other emotion related to fear such as anxiety, despair, embarrassment, insecurity, panic, or worry? Use this page to reflect back on that time or use this page the next time you get stuck on any of those emotions.

Try to relive that story, and complete the worksheet below to process through the experience. What or who triggered you? What happened?

S. **Stop**. After reading this short paragraph, close your eyes and visualize your "stuck" story. Imagine yourself taking a stop in that moment. Take some slow deep breaths and practice that stop here and now.

T. **Tell**. What does getting stuck on fear feel like? Can you feel that emotion in your body even now? Scan your body and identify the spot where you feel it. What does it feel like? Tightness? Achy? Burning? Notice that feeling(s). Write it down.

U. **Uncover**. What are your beliefs? Watch for words such as, "should", "always", "never" or other ways of describing how things are "supposed" to be? Reflect on each belief and check the accuracy of each of them. Write them down.

C. **Consider**. What can you consider now regarding the story? What consideration can you "take on?" Write that down.

K. **O.K.** Find compassion for yourself and remind yourself that it's O.K. to get stuck on something. If you are challenged to find compassion for yourself, consider what kind words you would say to a friend who got stuck. Replace his or her name with yours. Write that to yourself below.

Chapter 2: ANGER

Stuck on: Why Did You Lock Me Out of the House?

I went out with some friends the other night.

We attended a musical benefit raising money for a resident of a local community in need of assistance for cancer treatments.

It was a magical evening.

I left with a deep sense of gratitude for my health, family, and friends.

When I arrived home at midnight, my husband and children were sound asleep and the front door was locked.

I checked my pockets and my purse.

Nope. No keys.

Oh, man!

Why would my husband lock me out of the house knowing I wasn't in it?

Did he think I took my keys?

Why didn't he check the key rack?

If he had checked, he'd notice them hanging right where they belong!

Now what am I supposed to do?

I let out a sigh of defeat.

Hold yourself together, Shira.

Just call Boaz's cell phone.

Which I did.

But his phone was apparently turned off as the call went straight to his voice mail.

Call the house phone.

I did, but no one answered there either.

Because everyone was sleeping, of course!

I started knocking.

Nothing.

Argh!

Should I start screaming out my husband's name?

Would he even hear me?

So I cupped my hands and shouted toward the second floor:

"B-OOOOOOOO-AAAAAAAAA-ZZZZZZZZZZZ!"

Nothing.

I continued to call the house phone, knock on the door, and call out to my husband over the course of what felt like an hour, though it was probably something more like 10 minutes.

I felt my rage growing and growing.

How could he do this?

Does he not care about me?

At all?

I contemplated giving up and sleeping on the front stoop.

And then I thought twice about that.

Who are you kidding?

You're not going to sleep outside.

This is Boaz's fault!

And he needs to get out of bed and open the door for you!

I knew I was stuck, and I also knew that if I didn't process through it soon, the evening would turn from wonderful to terrible.

It already had.

So I stood still for a moment and **took a deep breath**.

*Shira, you're **stuck on anger**.*

I **uncovered** my very firm belief in that moment of how my husband should check if my keys are hanging on the key rack before he locks up at night and I am still out.

And if they are not, he should leave the house unlocked!

But as I reflected on what I believed my *husband* should do, I thought to myself that perhaps *I* should be giving him the benefit of the doubt.

Am I sure I didn't take my keys?

I checked again.

Nope, they're not on me.

As I looked up towards our bedroom and pictured my husband sound asleep, I **considered** to myself that while he may have been at fault here, it surely was an accident.

If anything, he was just trying to act responsibly by locking the house when he went to sleep.

And, perhaps, I should have compassion for having to wake him up after a long, hard work week.

And after one final, loud knock, my husband came to the door.

And instead of yelling, "Why did you lock me out?"

I whispered, "Sorry."

"What?" he asked rubbing his eyes.

"I'm sorry I had to wake you up."

And that was the end of it.

No fight.

No arguments.

No lecturing about "in the future."

I'll figure out what happened in the morning.

Which I did.

I told myself that I got stuck on anger, but that it's **O.K.**

And then, suddenly, my girlfriend called and told me she had found my keys on the back seat of her car.

Oh, man!

I couldn't believe what I heard.

I did take my keys? It was my own fault I was locked out?

Thankful I didn't blow up at my husband, I got ready for bed with the renewed sense of gratitude for my husband.

And grateful for The S.T.U.C.K Method.

Stuck on: You Did *What* to Your New Closet?

Today, I woke up with an itch to clean the house.

I started to straighten up the house right away.

My two youngest children were excited to join in.

"Can we help?"

"Uh, sure," I said. "Take these cloths and start dusting."

And off they went.

They dusted my bedroom.

They dusted the dining room.

They washed down the front of the refrigerator and the pantry closet.

"What next?" they asked eagerly.

"Uh, your room, I guess," I suggested.

"Go pick up your clothes off of the floor. Make your beds."

And off they went.

Two eager beavers.

It was a wonderful sight to see.

Because it doesn't happen too often.

Or ever, really.

And it made me happy.

After breakfast, I told them to get dressed and I would take them to the playground.

After I cleaned up the kitchen, one of my children called from his room because he needed some help getting dressed.

"Sure, here I come," I said with a hop and skip.

I looked at my 4-year-old son, who was only half dressed.

"How can I help you?" I asked.

"I can't reach my sweatshirt," he said pointing to his closet.

Sure.

No problem.

I turned around to open the closet.

The new custom-made closet.

The one with red crayon now drawn all over it.

"What is this?" I screamed.

My youngest son pointed to my third child, "He told me to do it."

"What?" I asked, looking at my third child. "Why would you tell him to color on your closet?"

"Because the closet was clean," he whispered innocently.

"Clean? What are you talking about?" I was dumbstruck.

"Well," he continued. "I couldn't clean the front of the closet because it was already clean. So we put crayon on it so that we could clean it up."

Did I just hear what I thought I heard?

Is this kid for real?

Furious, I yelled, "Well, clean it up! We are not leaving this house until all of that red is off!" I stormed out of their room.

And in that moment, I had a flashback to 1980, when I was 7 years old. My younger brother and I had innocently colored on the white walls of the living room of my parents' house.

With crayons.

Lots of them.

I won't ever forget that.

Because I remember getting yelled at.

And not quite understanding what I had done that was so

terrible.

And I also remember having to clean it up.

IMMEDIATELY!

Yikes!

Back to the present.

And still **stuck on anger** with my sons.

I didn't want to stay stuck.

So, I **walked out of the room** and took a deep breath.

I felt the anger in my heated face.

I counted to 10.

Slowly.

And **thought** about my belief that kids this age (4 and 7) should know by now that the only thing they are allowed to color on is paper.

Shouldn't they?

But as I paced around outside their room, I started to hear them giggle.

They weren't laughing at me.

They were having fun trying to scrub off the red crayon.

They turned it into a competition.

And I **considered** in that moment that my sons really had

no bad intentions.

I considered they really believed they would be able to clean it up when they started this whole thing, just as they had been successful in cleaning up the rest of the house.

I considered that they were just being creative, and creativity is something I honor and encourage in my kids.

What's really the big deal?

It's just a closet!

I went back into their room and observed my two boys working quite hard at getting the color off.

My frown turned into a smile.

I told them I was sorry I yelled at them.

And that I just reacted automatically in the moment.

And I reminded them we only color on paper, not furniture.

I got stuck on anger.

It happens.

Walking away from their room offered me the time and space I needed to reflect on what had just transpired.

And recognize the need to offer them an apology.

It also helped remind me that my kids are just kids.

And I'm really in no rush for them to grow up.

Stuck on: You Stupid, Stupid Driver!

The other day, on my way to drive my kids to their afterschool activities, I turned onto the road at the entrance to our neighborhood, and then soon came to a stop when I noticed the line of traffic up ahead of me.

But the woman in the car behind me was busy doing something else.

She didn't notice I had stopped.

Instead of slowing or stopping, she rammed right into the back of our car.

Which caused us to go into a 360-degree spin several times.

A nightmare.

A million times worse than the scariest amusement park ride you can imagine.

Because at least on a ride, you know when it will end.

We didn't, however.

Nor did we know if we would hit anything during our spin mid-road.

I honestly don't remember how many times we spun around exactly.

The truth is I don't remember much aside from the horrific screams of my three children in the car.

And my own screaming.

Immediately after our car came to a halt, I rushed to take off my seat belt and check that my kids were alive and breathing.

They were.

Thank God.

They were crying hysterically, but they were fine.

Our brand new car, on the other hand, was not.

It was totaled.

As I tried to calm them down and get them out of the car (the doors wouldn't open), I dialed my husband's cell phone with shaky hands.

Passersby came to help us.

I heard someone say something about the other driver using her phone at the time of the incident.

In seconds, I went from complete shock to complete anger.

What the %"%$%$?

Was she out of her mind?

Why was she on her cell phone while driving a car?

I was so **stuck on rage** at this stupid, stupid driver!

How dare she put my life and the life of my children in danger?!

I was beyond angry.

I was enraged.

I stared at her sitting on the ground holding her young child bleeding in her arms, and I wrapped my arms tighter around my frightened children.

How dare you?

I looked at her.

But she didn't look back.

She made no motion to come over to me to apologize.

And made no expressions of sorrow for having caused this accident.

My annoyance and fury grew.

The ambulances came.

The woman and her daughter got into one.

I was put on a stretcher and went into the other with my daughter.

(My husband arrived and took my two frightened sons, who seemed unharmed at the time, home.)

When the ambulance doors closed, I had an opportunity to **stop**.

I took one long deep breath.

A long, deep breath.

I told my daughter how I was **stuck on rage**.

I shared my **beliefs** that no one (NO ONE!) should be on their phones while driving a car!

And that the woman should have shown remorse or at least pretended to have cared about me and my children!

My daughter, also quite shaken up, listened to me.

We reflected upon maybe this other driver was in such a state of shock, like we were, that she wasn't able to reach out to us.

Together, we noted I had made no attempt to approach the other driver, either.

Then, somehow, we were able to **consider** that this was an accident, and accidents happen.

I got stuck on ~~anger~~ rage, but **I'm human**.

I'm still carrying many emotions with me, but I'm trying to hold them in bigger-picture thoughts, such as considering the miracle that we walked away nearly unscathed.

It, indeed, could have been a lot worse.

Stuck on: Catch the Baddies! Not Me!

One afternoon when I was driving my kids to their afterschool classes, I got pulled over by the police for not stopping at the stop sign at the edge of the *kibbutz* in which I live.

The thing is: I had stopped.

I just didn't count to "three-one thousand."

I probably only counted to "one-one thousand."

Or, truthfully, I didn't count at all. Or stop.

I just slowed down.

Looked left.

Saw no cars approaching.

And turned.

And that's when the young police officer appeared out of nowhere and signaled to me with his finger to pull over.

"Where are you from?" he asked in Hebrew.

"America?" I replied, in my naturally thick American accent, trying to be cute to divert attention from the matter.

He cocked his head.

"I mean, here," I stammered in Hebrew. "On the *kibbutz.* I live here. But, I'm from America. I'm a new immigrant."

"Well, immigrant or not, you didn't stop at that stop sign."

"I didn't?" I played on.

"No. You did not."

"Oh," I replied. "Are you sure? I always do."

He left me for a minute and walked to his police car, spoke to his colleague, and returned back to me to declare my violation.

250 shekels (about $80).

I started to cry. I could have stopped, but I also thought keeping it up might help my case.

"What are you crying for?"

"I just had two major abdominal surgeries, and I'm not working much, so I'm not earning much money and I'm such a good driver, and I'm an *American* driver, and I never, ever, ever had a violation in my life, and I don't deserve a ticket!"

I let it all out.

But he didn't care.

He's probably heard this many times before.

I wanted to continue with: *Don't you have anything else to do with your time?*

Why don't you catch the notorious drivers speeding and/or driving recklessly?

You should be catching the baddies! Not me!

But he went back to the car to write up his report.

It was a "natural" **stop** and I took advantage to breathe deeply for several minutes.

While I waited for the officer to return with my ticket, I **told** myself I was stuck on agitation.

I noticed a tightness in my stomach.

The more I breathed deeply, the more I noticed my stomach

muscles starting to relax.

I **thought** about what I really wanted to say, but upon reflection, I questioned who was I to be telling this officer how to do his job.

Do I even know what his daily work routine is? And whether or not he catches notorious drivers?

I **considered** that I had been in the wrong by not coming to a full stop.

And how this lesson may one day save my life.

Perhaps God's hand played in this scenario without my awareness.

I got stuck on agitation, but I was grateful that I didn't lash out at the cop when I know I could have.

I accepted my violation.

And I consoled myself, reminding myself it was **O.K.** that I got stuck on agitation in the first place.

And I drove a bit more carefully as I continued to take my kids to their afterschool activities.

Stuck on: The Kids Are Going to Miss the Bus!

Mornings in my house are challenging, because there's so much to do to get four kids out of bed, ready for school, and out the door by 7:25 a.m.

One morning, not too long ago, was particularly difficult.

It was 06:45 with T-minus 40 minutes and counting.

I woke up the two older kids.

The two younger ones were already awake.

My daughter, the oldest, got up easily.

My oldest son?

When I turned on the lights in his room and greeted him with a cheery, "Good morning!" he didn't respond.

He never does.

So, I stripped the bed of all its covers, at which point, he screamed, "NO!!!"

"LET. ME. SLEEP!"

Why, oh why, is this such a struggle every morning?

Perhaps I should be putting him to bed at 6 p.m. instead letting him stay up until 9 p.m.?

06:50.

T-minus 35 minutes and counting.

I had to get the kids dressed.

Thankfully, three of the four were able to do that reliably on their own.

But one claimed he didn't know how.

He knew.

He just didn't want to.

Instead, he chose to bury his face in the sofa and cry about it.

And while this hysterical scene was going on, another kid cried he couldn't find matching socks while another couldn't find one shoe.

"Well, shouldn't it be where it belongs?" I whined.

07:00.

T-minus 25 minutes and counting.

I needed some help around here.

I knew the kids were going to miss the bus.

"Boaz, where are you?" I called to my husband from the kitchen.

No answer.

So, I tried to stay on track without losing it.

It was time to make the ~~doughnuts~~ breakfast.

And hope my children would come to breakfast fully dressed.

One child wanted *this* bowl.

Another child wanted *that* spoon.

This one wanted *this* cereal, the other child wanted *that* one.

And this one just complained, "There's nothing ever to eat for breakfast in this house!"

Then, he went to the refrigerator, opened it, and stood there.

Staring.

He shut the refrigerator door empty-handed and returned to the table with a droopy face.

"There's nothing to eat," he mumbled.

07:10.

T-minus 15 minutes and counting.

As I continued with the morning routine, poured second helpings of cereal, picked up dropped spoons, and cleaned up spilled milk, I turned to look at the empty lunch boxes that needed to be filled.

But wait!

One child called, "Mommy! Wipe me!"

Why?

I don't know.

He's four.

But he still requests, and I still acquiesce.

But yikes!

The lunches still needed to be made!

And I was running out of time!

07:15!

T-minus 10 minutes and counting!

Three school lunches needed to be made.

And, of course, this one wanted a pita and that one wanted a roll.

This one wanted *tahini* and that one said he hates *tahini*.

This one preferred peanut butter and that one wanted jelly only.

I looked up again towards the second floor and called out to my husband, "Hello?????"

Anybody there????

I'm going a little crazy down here!

"I'd love some help!"

"I'm running out of time!"

"They're going to miss the bus!"

"BOOOOOOOOOOOOOOAAAAAAAAAAAAZZZZZZZZZ!?"

No answer.

07:20.

T-minus 5 minutes and counting.

As I frantically placed the lunches inside each school bag, I noticed some of the kids were still half dressed and some had dried milk all over their mouths and one still couldn't find his lost shoe, and, and ...

And I thought I was going to lose it ...

But guess who showed up?

Sauntered right in.

Cool as a cat.

All calm.

And refreshed.

Showered, shaved, dressed.

Smiling ear to ear.

He said, "I just put a load of laundry in. Don't forget to hang it, O.K.?"

WHAT?!?!?!?!?!?!?!?!?!

I didn't want to hear *that*.

I couldn't handle hearing *that*.

I started to cry.

And he stared at me skeptically.

"Are you okay? All I said was that I turned the laundry machine on."

And, I started to attack.

"Laundry? How can I think of laundry? I've got three kids needing to get to the bus, another kid needing to get to preschool, lunches half-made, bags not ready, a kitchen full of dishes ...

"And you're talking about *laundry*?"

WON'T. YOU. SHARE. MY. STRESS? I wanted to scream.

But I needed to get the kids out the door.

So I finished up with the kids, sent the older ones to school, and walked my youngest to preschool. When I came home, I **sat down at the kitchen table**, closed my eyes, and took a deep breath.

I was **stuck on agitation** at that point.

I felt it in my pounding heart.

I felt my shoulders rising towards my ears and as I continued to breathe, I noticed them starting to drop.

I **uncovered** my beliefs regarding the kids almost missing the bus and my husband playing no role in the family morning routine.

And that I carry all the morning stress alone.

How did this become my role?

But I knew those beliefs were unfounded.

My husband does help me on many mornings.

And I **considered** the kids have yet to miss the bus since they began going to school.

And I considered I don't *really* want my husband to share my stress.

He's got enough of it, with running his own business and

supporting a family of six.

And he certainly wouldn't want me to share the stress that he carries in his life.

And so instead, I asked him to help me figure out ways to reduce the morning stress in our household.

And we came up with a plan:

- Wake the kids up earlier.
- Teach them to prepare their *own* lunches in the morning (or even perhaps the night before).
- Help them pick out their clothes (if needed) before they go to bed and make sure their school bags are ready the night before.
- Remind them that we have a chalkboard hanging in the kitchen for a purpose: When we run out of their favorite food, write it down! I don't always notice what's missing.
- Encourage self-care with my youngest, including wiping his bottom (just like he does on his own at preschool).

My husband and I started implementing these ideas and suddenly, life became a lot less stressful in the mornings.

I got stuck on fear and agitation, but **I'm all right**. Being aware that I was stuck helped me move into a better routine.

I'm now able—most days—to respond to "I just put a load of laundry in" with a half-chuckle, smile, and a hug of gratitude.

Stuck on: But, You Said!

The other day my oldest son noticed a black lab puppy near the preschool on the *kibbutz*.

The puppy was standing alone, collarless, and shivering in the rain.

My son asked if we could take him home.

"Yes," I began. "Let's take him home, give him food, and start to put out notices to see if we can find the owner."

So we did.

We posted ads on local Google and Facebook groups.

We asked every passerby if they had any information on this lost dog.

When we learned no new information and became desperate, we asked people if they were interested in adopting this dog.

To no avail.

"I already have a dog."

"My house is too small."

"I don't like dogs."

"I don't want the responsibility."

And, in the meantime, the dog stayed with us.

And we all got attached to him.

"He's so cute!" my youngest son said.

"Can we keep the dog?" my second son pleaded.

"I'll take care of him!" my older son declared.

"The dog will make our family complete!" my daughter said.

And as a dog lover, I fell for all these terms of endearment.

Yes, this dog is adorable and will be a terrific addition to our six-person family.

I actually believed it would complete us.

So, I acquiesced.

Yes, one big, happy family!

Until, a week later, when the kids stopped taking care of the dog.

What's going on here?

You promised!

They complained about not having enough time to get ready for school *and* walk the dog in the morning.

So, as the only morning person in the family, I took on the responsibility to walk the dog.

Every morning.

But I soon realized my kids showed no interest in walking the dog in the afternoons or evenings either!

All of the responsibility suddenly fell into my lap!

How did this happen?

I never asked for this dog!

I have no time, nor energy for a fifth child!

Hearing my inner voice and my outside one (shouting at my kids), I soon could tell I was stuck.

So, I **took the dog outside for a walk**.

Getting out in the fresh air reminded me to take some deep breaths.

I noticed how I was **stuck on agitation** stemming from the desire to have a dog in the first place.

As I watched the puppy sniff around and do his thing, I **recalled** why I initially agreed to adopt the dog.

I thought it would complete my family!

What a joke!

And that my son said he was going to take 100% responsibility for it.

Apparently not!

I suddenly **considered** all the expenses and other implications of adopting this dog I initially ignored when I was blinded by puppy love.

After a few heart-to-hearts with my children, we made a choice to give the dog away to another family.

Fortunately, this other family lived across the street from us.

So, my kids were lucky to able to visit the dog as often as they wanted.

It really was a win-win situation for all.

I loved the puppy and the idea of having a dog in our family. Yet, the reality brought agitation.

That's **O.K.**

Processing this helped me realize how love and desire can be so blinding.

We're not ready for a dog now, but maybe someday.

For now, we'll enjoy the puppy who lives across the street.

Open Workbook Pages – Stuck on Anger

Can you think of a time you were stuck on anger or any other emotion related to anger such as: agitation or rage? Use this page to reflect back on that incident or use this page the next time you get stuck on any of those emotions. I urge you to take the opportunity to be vulnerable, identify the emotions they feel, and process through them.

Try to relive that story and complete the worksheet below to process through the experience. What or who triggered you? What happened?

S. **Stop**. After reading this short paragraph, close your eyes and visualize your "stuck" story. Imagine yourself taking a stop in that moment. Take some slow deep breaths and practice that stop here and now.

T. **Tell**. What does getting stuck on anger feel like? Can you feel that emotion in your body even now? Scan your body and identify the spot where you feel it? What does it feel like? Tightness? Achy? Burning? Notice that feeling(s). Write it down.

U. **Uncover**. What were are beliefs in this particular story? Watch for words such as: "should have", "always", "never", or other ways of describing how things are "supposed" to be. Reflect on your beliefs and check the accuracy of each of them. Write them down.

C. **Consider**. What can you consider now regarding the story? What consideration can you "take on?" Write them down.

K. **O.K.** Find compassion for yourself and remind yourself that it's O.K. to get stuck on something. Write that to yourself below.

Chapter 3: AVERSION

Stuck on: No Exercise Will Make Me Happy!

As a kid, I exercised a lot.

But I never called it "exercise."

I called it "playing out in the backyard," or "dancing in the basement," or "playing basketball," or "fishing for pennies at the bottom of a pool."

They weren't things I *had* to do.

They were things I did because they were *fun!*

The joy I received from doing them motivated me.

And no matter what form of so-called "exercise" I did, I was in heaven when I was doing it.

I loved sweating.

I loved the high of getting my heart rate up.

I loved the feeling afterward of being tired and hungry for a wholesome meal.

But now I live on a small *kibbutz* in the middle of nowhere with no gym nearby (where I would swim laps or take yoga classes).

And I don't feel uninhibited enough to just go outside and play on the *kibbutz* playground alongside the children.

(Even though I totally want to some days.)

Therefore, I feel limited with my exercise options.

So, I took up jogging.

Because I had to choose *something* to get my heart rate up.

Even if jogging is the most boring thing in the world.

See, this is what happens when you become an adult.

Exercise becomes boring!

I hated every aspect of the jogging routine.

I hated putting on running shoes.

I hated being cold and bundled up at 5:30 a.m., stripping off layer by layer as I broke into a sweat, and then having to carry my extra clothing while jogging up and down the hills of the *kibbutz*.

I really hate jogging.

I'm so bad at it.

I can only run eight minutes without stopping anyway.

Really, what's the point?

So, I took up walking instead.

Which, with captivating podcasts to listen to I found walking more pleasant. (Thank you, "Happier" with Gretchen Rubin, "On Being" with Krista Tippett, "Small Changes Big Shifts" with Dr. Michelle Robin, and "The Highly Sensitive Person Podcast" with Kelly O'Laughin.)

In fact, I cherished the stillness at dawn, the majestic view of the Nazareth mountains and the idyllic tranquility of the Eshkol reservoir.

But it wasn't enough.

I wasn't getting my heart rate up enough and I wasn't sweating.

It wasn't elevating my mood either.

I mean, maybe it could have "worked", if I had pushed myself to walk faster.

But if I'm gonna push myself, why not just go back to jogging?

But, I despise jogging!

With a passion!

So I stopped exercising completely, because I knew no exercise would satisfy me.

Until the other day, when I noticed my daughter dancing around the living room with her favorite music accompanying her in the background.

It was obvious she was in heaven.

Just like I had been, when I danced around in the basement of my parents' home when I was a kid.

And she was *exercising*!

And sweating.

And getting her heart rate up.

With a passion!

Oh, how I despise jogging!

As I sat down on the couch and watched my daughter dance, I felt my whole tense body sink into the sofa and I recognized I was **stuck on aversion**.

I **thought** about my belief that exercise has to become boring once you become an adult and I immediately caught my distorted thinking.

It dawned on me in that moment that, even though I am an adult, exercising does not *have* to be boring!

It can still be *fun*!

I **considered** that I, too, could take up dancing again as an alternative way to exercise.

I could dance in my living room, just like my daughter does.

And that is just what I chose to do.

The next day, I searched for Latin music on YouTube, cleared the living room, turned up the volume, and *danced*.

At one point, I even closed my eyes and pretended to be auditioning for a spot on "Dancing with the Stars," professionally led by some beautiful man who knew how to turn and flip me in inconceivable ways!

And there I was.

Sweating and getting my heart rate up and *enjoying* every minute.

I got stuck on despising jogging, but I held myself in **compassion** and became grateful for the discovery that came from it.

And for the newly formed morning dance group that emerged from it.

Stuck on: Your Group Activity is Tasteless!

I participated in a women's personal growth group a few years ago in my community.

We met twice a month alternating hosting in our respective homes.

Each time, another woman facilitated and I always looked forward to learning and experiencing something new.

Most evenings were focused on some kind of creative self-development activity, like when one of my friends divided us into partners one night and instructed us to take turns asking and answering the following two questions about our respective partners, after which we were encouraged to offer our partner a blessing:

1) What do you like about your partner?
2) What do you find difficult about your partner?

From the get-go, I felt uncomfortable about this activity.

I mean, really, I'm supposed to sit across from my friend and tell her what I find difficult about her?

Really?

There's no way I would do that!

There's no way I could do that!

But I couldn't escape.

I mean, I didn't really *want* to escape.

I just felt uncomfortable.

So, during the first round, to make this a bit more comfortable for me, I asked my partner to go first.

It was a wise choice.

My friend told me lots of things she liked about me, found nothing difficult about me, and offered me a beautiful blessing.

Well, that was easy!

She finds nothing difficult about me?

If I had only known!

Moreover, I felt relieved because I felt no pressure to confront her with the things I found difficult about her!

This will be a piece of cake!

After the first round, the leader divided us up again and the second round was similar to the first.

I was relaxed by this point in the evening.

Then, she divided us into pairs for the final time.

And I was paired up with *her*.

The leader!

Uh-oh!

Time for trouble!

She went first:

"What do I like about you, Shira? I love how you are a leader in our community. I love your creativity, the calm presence you bring to others, and your wisdom. I love how you are friendly with so many different people in our community. You don't seem to be part of one clique or another. I love your kids and how you parent them."

"Thank you," I replied, with cautious sincerity.

"What do I find difficult about you? Well, you are a beautiful person, but you walk around our community without putting much effort at all into how you look. Truthfully, you look like a *shlump* most of the time, walking around in sweatpants and old t-shirts. You've been wearing the same clothes for the past six years! You never wear makeup. Like I said, you are beautiful, but you don't show the world your beauty."

"My blessing for you is blah, blah, blah, blah..."

I was so stuck on her temerity that I couldn't pay attention to her blessing.

Did I hear what I think I heard?

She doesn't like how I dress?

Did she really say that?

What nerve!

She has no right to tell me that!

I didn't show my emotions, though.

At least, I don't think I did. But, maybe I did.

Outwardly, I accepted her words with a forced smile, but inside my heart was beating a thousand times a minute.

I have no recollection of what I said to her when it was my turn to share my thoughts about her, though I'm confident I was not honest about the feelings I held towards her.

I was too stunned.

Too stung, in fact.

Too hurt.

And too averse to this ridiculous activity!

I knew from the moment this evening started it wasn't going to turn out well.

I walked around for the next few days thinking how stupid the activity had been.

A few days later, I bumped into the leader and she asked how I enjoyed the evening.

It turned out to be a natural **stop.**

This time, I was honest.

I **told** her I felt uneasy with it.

I told her I didn't like hearing things my friends find difficult about me.

I **thought** about how instead of uplifting others, this activity had the potential to make people feel terrible about themselves.

I **thought** about how, instead of an opportunity to connect, this activity could cause people to distance themselves from one another.

Yet, my friend helped me explore the accuracy of my beliefs.

She expressed to me that this activity is the most valued of all the group activities in her off-the-*kibbutz* spirituality group.

She said she even implements this activity with her husband on occasion, for bonding and relationship strengthening.

This led me to **consider** that perhaps there was more to the activity than I was willing to see.

I considered that the leader, who had been the only one in the group who was genuinely upfront with me, was simply trying to act as a mirror and show me a perspective that she had assumed I never noticed before.

She was actually trying to *empower* me.

And the change that I could ultimately initiate on hearing this reflection might lift me up, not bring me down.

I **considered** this activity could actually strengthen a friendship.

The truth is, I dress exactly the way she described me.

I do look like a *shlump* most of the time.

And while I certainly don't need to change my ways for any person other than myself, and I could also consider her words have no merit, I could try to dress nicer once in a while and perhaps by doing so, I'd feel better about myself.

So I did.

I thought about how I got stuck on uneasiness.

I was so averse to this activity at the time that I couldn't see the value in it.

But, it's **O.K.**

To this day, I am grateful to my friend, who took the risk to be authentic with me and empowered me to open my mind to new ways of seeing.

Stuck on: Why Doesn't Our Community Have Rules?

A few days ago, my children and I participated in an event at our community garden—an afternoon of pulling weeds, making pita on the fire, and eating vegetables straight out of our plots.

With the email invitation came a request we bring materials from our homes for the event: large bowls, flour, salt, cooking pans, knives, onions, and spades.

My children and I were the first to arrive, materials in hand: a large bowl, two packages of flour, and salt.

We were ready to start!

As one of the adults started the fire and another adult started chopping the vegetables she had just picked from her plot, my kids made dough from the flour we brought.

Within minutes, our dough was ready.

My children took small pieces of the dough, rolled them into balls, and patted them down into pancake-like pieces.

They placed each one on the hot pan.

Some of the other kids noticed the bowl of dough I was holding.

"Can I have some dough?" one kid asked.

"Sure," I said with an open heart.

"Can I?" another kid asked.

"Sure," I said with a smile.

"Can I?" a third one asked.

"All right," I said, but I began to notice my annoyance and my heart beginning to close.

What's going on here?

Am I the dough provider?

This isn't fair!

Why should I be giving out all my flour to every kid here?

What about the other parents?

Where's their dough?

Why can't others be responsible like I am?

I couldn't even enjoy the beautiful event.

As the sun started to set and everyone began to clean up, I **stopped** to take a conscious breath and then I approached the organizer of the event to share my feelings. I was still feeling **stuck on annoyance**, but I had a hunch that talking it through with someone might be a good way to help me consider my beliefs. I wasn't quite able to get there on my own yet.

First, I acknowledged the organizer for her efforts, and then I shared with her my feelings about what I **perceived** as disorganization of the event.

I explained what happened with the dough.

I told her I felt as if I was the only one working that afternoon.

She acknowledged me, and at the same time, gently helped me realize my beliefs weren't 100% accurate.

She helped me noticed all the people who took part in the event:

Those who organized it, those who made and cared for the fire, the person who brought the cooking pan and olive oil, the person who brought the knife and cutting board, those who cut and shared vegetables from their own garden, the person who cut up the vegetables, and the people who cooked the vegetables and the pita on the fire.

I **considered** in that moment how my children and I benefited from the good-heartedness of others in our community.

I also began to consider how closed-hearted I was that day and how in the future, I may be able to open my heart a bit more so as not to allow emotions to overcome me and ruin the experiences I am in.

I got stuck on annoyance.

But it's **O.K.,** because it reminded me that when I get stuck in my own story, I should remember there's always another story out there to consider. And often times our friends or family are available to help bring that awareness to us.

Stuck on: Nail Polish Remover Stinks!

I flew with my daughter to Eilat, a beach resort town, for a three-day getaway last winter.

Shortly after boarding the plane, I closed my eyes for a few minutes while half listening to the flight attendant provide directions regarding safety protocol.

I was hoping to doze off, but I was forced to open my eyes instead.

Something stank!

Agh!

What in the world is that smell?

I turned to the lady sitting on my left and noticed she was dipping her fingers into a jar of liquid.

Nail polish remover!

Is this woman for real?

If there's one smell I can't stand (besides nail polish itself), it is nail polish remover.

"Will you please close that?" I asked in the most polite way possible, without saying outright how audacious she was for bringing nail polish remover on a plane in the first place!

"Oh. Sure. Is this bothering you?" she replied kindly.

I stopped in my tracks because her kindness made me **pause**.

I noticed **how annoyed I felt** and I noticed many **thoughts** running through my mind, such as this lady's insensitivity in opening nail polish remover on board.

Can I really call this lady insenstitive?

I **considered** perhaps she wasn't bothered by the smell of nail polish remover and therefore, assumed no one else would be either.

She probably just didn't even think about it.

She most likely had no bad intentions.

As I sat there, held hands with my daughter, and waited for the plane to take off, I thought about how I get stuck on annoyance sometimes. I thought, too, about how this is a trigger for me, but it's **O.K.** I realized how I am getting better at more quickly noticing my triggers, stopping, and considering other beliefs. I felt grateful in that moment ... and suddenly the smell began to subside.

Stuck on: You Won't Let Me Atone for My Sins?

In preparation for the holy day of Yom Kippur this year, I adopted a practice of approaching at least three people in my community to ask for forgiveness from them.

A month before the holiday, I approached the first person and he seemed to pay attention carefully to my words of apology.

He in turn asked for a general forgiveness from me.

I was happy.

When I approached the second community member, however, he responded by saying, "We don't have a deep or intimate enough relationship to have this conversation."

Huh?

Did I hear what I thought I just heard?

Is this person for real?

I wanted to apologize to him in sincerity, and he won't allow me the opportunity?!

I replied with a quiet "O.K." before walking away, even though I wasn't clear at all on what transpired.

This interaction did *not* make me happy.

I communicated with the third community member via email and asked to set up a time to speak in person.

She replied, "I'm busy. Can you just tell me what you want in writing?"

So, I wrote that it was related to *Yom Kippur* and asking for forgiveness, and I'd rather meet in person.

I waited for a response.

But, she never responded.

What a disappointment!

How could this be?

How could she?

Two out of three people turned me down.

And did not let me atone for my sins!

Or make amends!

What nerve!

How could they?

But a few minutes after I noticed all of these thoughts racing through my head and noticed how emotional I was, I **stopped**.

I closed my eyes and took some breaths.

I **told** myself I was stuck on annoyance.

And looked at my **belief**.

That these people have a religious obligation to participate in my atonement activity on my terms, the way I want, how I want and when I want.

Do they? Really?

But, then I **considered** that perhaps my approach was unconventional and could even possibly make others uncomfortable.

I **considered** not everyone is interested to participate in my traditions.

I accepted that perspective and moved on.

And then **forgave myself.**

Just before Yom Kippur.

The perfect day.

Open Workbook Pages – Stuck on Aversion

Can you think of a time you were stuck on aversion or any other emotion related to aversion such as: annoyance or uneasiness? Use this page to reflect back on it or go through the following steps the next time you get stuck on any of those emotions. I urge you to take the opportunity to be vulnerable, identify the emotions they feel, and process through them.

Try to relive that story and complete the worksheet below to process through the experience. What or who triggered you? What happened?

_____

_____

_____

_____

_____

_____

_____

_____

_____

_____

_____

S. **Stop**. After reading this short paragraph, close your eyes and visualize your "stuck" story. Imagine yourself taking a stop in that moment. Take some slow deep breaths and practice that stop here and now.

T. **Tell**. What does getting stuck on aversion feel like? Can you feel that emotion in your body? Scan your body and identify the spot where you feel it? What does it feel like? Does it bring about nausea? Headache? Notice that feeling. Write it down.

_____

_____

_____

_____

_____

_____

_____

U. **Uncover**. What are your beliefs in this particular story? Watch for words such as: "should have", "always", "never", or other ways of describing how things are "supposed" to be. Reflect on your beliefs and check the accuracy of each one. Write them down.

_____

_____

_____

_____

_____

_____

_____

C. **Consider**. What can you consider now regarding the story? What consideration can you "take on?" Write it down.

K. **O.K.** Find compassion for yourself and remind yourself that it's O.K. to get stuck on something. Notice even how you could have stayed stuck longer than you did, but did not. Write words of compassion and kindness to yourself below.

SHIRA TAYLOR GURA

Chapter 4: PRIDE

Stuck on: I Am Better than You

Monday afternoons are challenging for me.

I drive my kids to various extracurricular activities, drop one kid off here, drop another kid off there, do a food shop in between, pick one kid up, pick the other kid up, and then finally head home.

It's exhausting, and by the time we return home, it's nearly 7 p.m.

When I walk into the house with my packages, it's never quite clear if my other two children, who stayed home with my husband, have eaten dinner or not.

Last night, I came home famished and noticed there was no dinner on the table.

I asked my husband if he could make a quick salad, which he generously agreed to.

As I was putting the groceries away, I heard my husband tell the kids the salad was ready.

Yet, no one came to the kitchen to eat.

"It looks like no one wants to eat," he said to me.

"Great," I responded. "A quiet dinner just for the two of us."

We just started eating when our 5-year-old approached the island in our kitchen. He started bouncing up and down yelling, "I want salad! I want salad!"

"Okay," I responded, "So sit down!"

But he kept bouncing.

And then accidently hit his head on the corner of the island.

Agh!

He started to scream.

And so did I.

I turned to my husband and whined, "Why did you say the kids don't want to eat? If I were in charge, I would have forced them to sit down to eat!"

Dumbfounded, he responded defensively, "What's the connection between whether or not the kids came to the table to eat and the fact that Amir just hit his head? Are you trying to blame me for Amir getting hurt?"

Feeling the situation escalating, I responded in an extremely calm voice, "You don't need to yell at me."

"But, why do you do that?" he continued to insist.

And all during this exchange, our son was still screaming and receiving no attention.

So, I turned to him and gave him some ice and a big hug.

Our son calmed down within seconds, climbed up to his bar stool, and began eating.

But, my husband and I weren't done.

"Can we talk about what just happened?" my husband initiated.

"No, I'd rather not talk to you right now," I replied.

"Well, I would like to talk about it," he insisted. "Now."

Frustrated with his insistence, I **stopped**, closed my eyes, and quickly reflected on the incident in my mind. I recognized I was **stuck on self-righteousness**.

I **believed** my son hit his head because my husband did not insist he come to the table to eat.

What kind of logic is that, Shira?

One has nothing to do with the other!

And I **considered** I was wrong for blaming my husband for it.

"Look. I got stuck. I'm sorry. Can we move on with our lives?" I pleaded.

"Ah. An apology. It's all I wanted to hear," he said.

Hmph.

And then I began to cry right into my bowl of salad.

Not because of my husband's behavior, but because I was disappointed for getting stuck in the first place.

And then I suddenly remembered step "K."

I missed it!

In that moment, I held myself in compassion and told myself that it was **O.K.** I got stuck on self-righteousness, and that while I have the best intentions in life to slow down my lightning-fast reactivity, I don't always succeed, because I'm not perfect.

With that, I felt grateful for my husband for accepting my apology and blessed for having the tools to be able to get unstuck and move on with my life.

Stuck on: My Grey

People were looking at me.

Or at least that's the feeling I was getting when I arrived to my NJ hometown on my annual summer family visit.

It began when I sensed someone looking at the top of my head.

Why is he looking up there?

Do I have lice up there?

Over the next couple of days, I felt more of the same behavior from others.

Am I begin self-conscious?

My hair, no longer covered by a scarf, as I had been wearing for religious purposes, now revealed something about me that was hidden to others for several years: my grey.

My hunches were confirmed when I overheard my 5-year-old nephew ask, "Why does Shira's hair look different from everyone else's?"

And when I relayed what I thought was a funny story to my

sister, she admitted her teenage son had asked a similar question.

Yet, his was more direct.

"Why does Shira have grey hair?" she relayed to me.

And her response back to him was, "Well, most older people do. They just cover it with color, so you don't see it."

Yikes!

My hunches were true!

People *were* staring at me.

Or rather, at my grey hair.

Even though *I* had already noticed my own grey (salt-and-pepper, really) and embraced it, I did look different from the rest of the adults my age. Still young at 41, I looked old.

Which made me wonder:

Am I stuck on keeping this grey hair?

And if yes, why?

Why have I chosen up until this point never to color my hair?

I mulled over this for a few days, and then chose **to go for a swim** – one of my favorite **stops**.

As I stepped into the water, I noticed I don't quite like that feeling when the cool water meets my not-so-warm body. I also noticed I was **stuck on rigidity**.

As I started my laps, I uncovered my **beliefs**:

Natural is beautiful.

Grey is beautiful!

Natural is the only way!

Our society is wrong in its view of a woman's natural beauty as unattractive.

As I continued to lift my head out of the water for a breath of air every few seconds, I reflected on my beliefs.

Is natural always the right way?

I **wondered** if perhaps women color their hair, not necessarily to conform to society's view, but to feel better about themselves.

And I **wondered** if feeling good about oneself is something that shouldn't be underrated.

I **could** try to color my hair, just once, (and with a natural product, of course), and see how I respond to it.

So, I did.

And lo and behold …

I liked it.

In fact, I loved it!

It made me look youthful: closer to how I feel about myself.

So, I decided that for the 41-year-old me I am today, this is how I'd like to look for now.

A brunette.

A young-looking, full-of-life brunette.

And someday, I'll go back to my beautiful grey.

I got stuck on rigidity, but **I'm fine**.

I realized that when I was stuck, my outlook was narrow.

Even though I previously liked my grey hair, I learned I could like change even better.

Change of my own choosing.

Stuck on: You Have No Heart!

I woke up this morning and witnessed two birds building a nest outside our kitchen window.

I was awestruck of God's miracles and excited to show my children this magnificent scene.

They were equally amazed and after they left for school, I even thought about documenting it all on video as a surprise for when they would return home.

My 3-year-old was apparently so impressed by the nest that he told his teacher and classmates all about it. She subsequently chose to walk the class over to our house during their morning outing in hopes that I would be home and could show the children the scene.

When the class arrived, I welcomed them in, and instructed them to walk quietly to the kitchen.

Over at the window, I picked up each child, one by one, so

they could each watch the birds at work.

Nature as your classroom!

An unforgettable educational experience!

A few minutes later, the kids returned to their preschool and I went back to work at the computer.

About 15 minutes later, I heard a noise in the kitchen.

I called out to my husband, who had walked in the house just as the preschool kids were leaving, and asked if he knew what that sound was.

"I just got rid of a bird nest that was forming outside our window," he answered matter-of-factly.

You WHAT?

"YOU WHAT?" I yelled out loud at him.

"How could you destroy an animal's habitat? Have you no heart at all?"

My husband responded defensively.

"What? You want a nest on our kitchen windowsill?" he asked incredulously. "What about all the diseases birds carry?" he continued. "You want that coming into our house? And what are you so excited about anyway? There are a zillion trees in the area. Why can't those birds just build a nest in the tree *next* to our house instead of right outside our kitchen window?"

I made a face at him and stormed out of the kitchen.

I was angry. I could feel it in every muscle in my back and shoulders.

My head felt like it was about to explode.

I **stopped**. I counted to 10.

My husband is so heartless!

He never consults with me on important matters!

I counted to 10 again.

After the second set of 10 breaths, I realized that besides anger, I was **stuck on being holier-than-thou**.

I **believed** my husband, unlike me, has no heart.

Really?

I **considered** that my husband didn't know I was planning to document the building of this nest.

And that this issue wasn't really an important life matter in the scheme of things.

And that maybe my husband had a point.

Having a bird nest on our kitchen windowsill may not be the best idea.

I accepted that my husband didn't do anything intentional to hurt or spite me and apologized for yelling at him, which he accepted.

I got stuck on **holier than thou**, but it's **O.K**.

Processing through it allowed me to realize that as much as I wanted to protect that little bird nest, I also needed to protect the nest I already have at home and worked quite hard to build.

And staying stuck on the bird nest certainly wasn't going to help that.

Stuck on: You Have No Plans on Apologizing?

My child got hurt last week.

Rush-to-the-hospital hurt.

Stiches-in-the-head hurt.

Due to a rock thrown at her head.

By another child.

In our community.

Unintentionally, of course.

When we returned from the hospital, the parents of the child knocked on our door and said, "Our child is really sorry for what he did. It was an accident."

The child is sorry?

Is this an acceptable form of an apology?

How do we know your child is sorry?

Why isn't he here to tell us in his own words?

Something is wrong with this situation!

The kid *is supposed to apologize on his own.*

I want that child to come over now and apologize to my son!

I looked over at my son sitting in the living room with bandages on his head.

I was boiling.

But I said nothing about that.

I solemnly thanked the parents for coming over and closed the door. I did not feel satisfied by this apology and noticed the tightness in my face and shoulders.

I let out a huff and **sat down on the couch** with my son.

I closed my eyes and took a deep breath.

I expressed to my son my **judgmental feelings**.

I told my son I **believed** had this situation been reversed, he would have apologized.

Because I would have taught him so.

The right way.

The only way.

Or, so I thought.

Is there really one right way?

But as I looked at my son, who didn't seem to flinch when the child didn't show up at the door with his parents, I **considered** that there may have been more to the story.

Perhaps, it takes this other child more time to process than other children, and perhaps he will apologize to my son, but in his own time and in his own way.

Not *my* way.

And perhaps I need to accept that.

For now, my son did receive an apology and for that I am grateful.

I got stuck on judgment, but it's **O.K.**

I acknowledged out loud, in front of my son, the relief I felt by receiving a genuine apology from the boy's parents, even though the feeling of disappointment lingered for a few more days.

Stuck on: Help! My Child is Drowning!

A few weeks ago, I participated in Israel's largest amateur sports event—the annual swim across the Sea of Galilee.

It was an exciting event to be a part of, along with approximately 12,000 other people from all over the country and the world.

And it was exhilarating, after a grueling but invigorating 2½-hour swim to reach the finish line, where hundreds of people line up to greet and congratulate their loved ones.

I became curious about whether my husband would be one of those people waiting at the finish line.

When my feet were able to touch the bottom of the sea, I

took off my goggles and started to walk out of the water.

With the sun in my eyes, I squinted and searched around for my husband.

I couldn't see him.

I assumed he was just busy taking care of the kids.

A good father.

Suddenly I spotted him.

He wasn't standing along the shoreline with the other people waiting to greet the swimmers.

He was wading in the water.

He looked as if he were searching for something.

His hands were cupped over this mouth, as if he were calling out to someone.

What is he doing?

I ran toward him.

His arms were not open to congratulate me, and his face did not show any signs of pride.

He looked scared for his life.

"I can't find Avi Chai," he said out of breath.

Words I will never forget.

"You what?" I responded, breathless – both from having completed this intense swim and also in disbelief for what I had just heard.

"What do you mean you can't find Avi Chai?" I went on.

"Weren't you watching him?"

"And, why are you here in the water and not up at the campground searching for him?"

Until the answer to my question came to me.

My husband had already searched the campground.

He scoped it out completely.

I know him well.

He was here, in the water, because he believed that maybe our son made his way down to it.

A 3-year old.

Who doesn't even know how to swim.

Oh. My. God!

My heart stopped.

I cursed at my husband a whole bunch of times while I called out to my missing son and searched the water for a floating body.

I was sure my son drowned.

I searched frantically.

I yelled to my husband to also search frantically.

We engaged the police's help.

The search lasted for about 10 minutes.

Ten of the scariest minutes of my life.

And then, out of nowhere, my husband and I found him.

Sitting next to a friend, watching a children's performance at the main stage of the event.

I ran to him, squeezed him tightly, and started to cry.

"Are you O.K.?" I cried a few times.

"Ema! Shhhh! I can't hear!"

He was fine.

Then, I turned to my husband and went back to yelling at him.

"What were you doing this whole time, if not watching our children? Any responsible parent would never lose his child!" I said, judgmentally. "What kind of father are you?"

I **stopped** when my husband softly replied, "I was watching him. I was watching all the kids."

I took a deep breath.

I noticed how I was **stuck on being judgmental**.

My husband opened his arms for a hug.

In his arms, sobbing with relief, I recognized how I believed he was an irresponsible parent and was blinded in the moment to the fact that my belief was completely inaccurate.

I **considered** that losing a child can happen to anyone.

And that losing a child has nothing to do with what kind of father my husband is.

As I held my husband tight, I recognized that accidents happen.

To even the best of us.

And I also recognized we all get stuck.

And it's **O.K.**

I apologized for yelling at him.

And thanked God my child was found alive.

And that my husband and I were able to move on with our day.

Without anger (or fear) between us.

Open Workbook Pages – Stuck on Pride

Can you think of a time that you were stuck on pride or any other emotion related to pride such as: holier than thou, judgment, pride, self-righteousness, rigidity? Use this page to reflect back on it or use this page the next time you get stuck on being right.

Try to relive that story and complete the worksheet below to process through the experience. What or who triggered you? What happened?

_____

_____

_____

_____

_____

_____

_____

_____

_____

_____

S. **Stop**. After reading this short paragraph, close your eyes and visualize your "stuck" story. Imagine yourself taking a stop in that moment. Take some slow deep breaths and practice that stop here and now.

T. **Tell.** What does getting stuck on pride feel like? Can you feel that emotion in your body? Scan your body and identify the spot where you feel it. In your belly? In your neck? Notice it. Write it down.

_____

_____

_____

_____

_____

_____

_____

U. **Uncover.** What are your beliefs in this particular story? Watch for words such as: "should have", "always", "never", or other ways of describing how things are "supposed" to be? Reflect on your beliefs and check the accuracy of them. Write them down.

_____

_____

_____

_____

_____

_____

_____

_____

C. **Consider**. What can you consider now regarding the story? What consideration can you "take on?" Write it down.

K. **O.K.** Find compassion for yourself and remind yourself that it's O.K. to get stuck on something. What kind words would you say to a friend who got stuck? Write that to yourself below.

Chapter 5: GLOOM

Stuck on: Shame on Me!

Not long ago, our community held an event honoring residents for their volunteer work.

I was out of the country at the time, but I understood from my husband, who attended the event, that my name wasn't mentioned.

I wasn't given any honor.

No recognition.

Even though I volunteer on nearly every committee; even though I selflessly put my community before myself and my family.

Boy, was I pissed off!

Minutes later, I received a message from my mother who shared the devastating news of the loss of someone I had gone to high school with.

The sister of my classmate.

The daughter of my parents' good friends.

An occupational therapist, like me.

Lindsey.

A wonderful, dynamic, and inspirational person who lost a battle to cancer.

"Someone who was dealt a shitty hand, faced it with grace and humor, fought like a warrior, and refused to wallow even once in 11 years," wrote one friend on her Facebook page.

"Someone who will be remembered for her beaming positive energy," wrote another.

An "enthusiastic" person.

An "incredibly special" person.

Taken away too young.

And suffered way too much.

And here I am disappointed that I wasn't acknowledged at some stupid community event!

Shame on me!

And shame on me for getting stuck in all my other mundane and frivolous matters!

And blogging about those experiences!

While others in the world are really suffering!

Maybe I should just terminate my blog?

Then at least the world won't know the small things I sweat.

I'll just keep them to myself.

I mean really, the world has enough problems in it without me having to air my dirty laundry out there, right?

I stood up and walked away from the computer.

How can I possibly blog in this moment?

That wouldn't be the right thing to do!

I went for a walk and got a breath of fresh air.

I thought about the bereaved family.

I couldn't even imagine the pain they were in.

How are they going to be able to move on from this?

I started to tear up.

And cry for the family's loss.

And for my own shame.

And then out of nowhere, my cell phone beeped, an external **stop**.

I opened it and saw I received another email.

It came from one of my blog subscribers.

As I wiped my tears away, I read this man's personal "stuck story" and how he claimed he was able to get through his situation with the help of the tools he had learned from my blog.

Amazing.

I looked up from my phone and reminded myself a few moments ago I was **stuck on shame**.

There I was, contemplating terminating my blog, **believing** it was worthless, and then I received this email reaffirming the place it holds in this world.

Processing through this situation helped me **consider** that everyone has his or her own stories and none of them are more or less trivial than another.

They are all important.

Because they belong to us and form who we are.

I got stuck on shame, but I held myself in **compassion**.

Processing through it helped me recognize that even during a time of someone else's loss, I can still write.

Knowing that my sharing has a value in this world.

Stuck on: I'm Not Good Enough

My mother-in-law invited me for coffee the other day.

She said she's had something on her mind for a while that she's been wanting to say to me.

And that with the new year approaching, it was a good time as ever to share it.

I wondered what this was all about.

Maybe she wants to apologize to me?

Actually, I couldn't have been farther from the truth.

Instead, she spoke to me about how we've grown apart.

How I used to call more often.

How I used to check up on her more often.

How we used to go out for coffee.

And now, there's none of that.

What are you talking about?

What does this mean?

That I'm not good enough?

How dare you?!

Don't you know how much is already on my plate?

Now I need this guilt trip?

Really?

This made me feel so sad, I wanted to cry.

I wanted to lash out at her, but I kept my thoughts to myself.

Noticing the negative thoughts racing through my mind and my clenched fists, I knew I was stuck.

As difficult as it was in that moment, I **closed my eyes** and took several deep breaths.

I told myself I was **stuck on gloom**.

I thought about my **belief** that my mother-in-law has no right to judge me and that she should keep her opinions to herself.

But, upon reflection, I wondered who am I to say what she should or should not do.

And then **considered** that I'm not always a perfect person— no one is—and that perhaps my mother-in-law was trying to tell me something deeper, beyond these words.

Perhaps she was lonely and looking for company.

Perhaps she missed me.

And I could be doing a bit more to recognize that and show my love to her.

Maybe she has a point?

I considered I could be picking up the phone more often, or inviting her to coffee more regularly.

Which is what I chose to do.

And I told her.

Instead of crying, I embraced her.

In a matter of minutes I moved from gloom to compassion for her.

And **compassion** towards myself.

In fact, since that conversation, I have felt even more grateful my mother-in-law was brave enough to speak to me from her heart, and that she helped me remember that I'm not a perfect person.

That takes an act of extreme courage.

Courage and compassion — both great lessons going into the new year.

Stuck on: What an Attitude!

I was at a community potluck meal recently and as it came to a close, most people in attendance helped clean up.

Out of the corner of my eye, I noticed a friend of mine ask one of the teenagers, a friend of my daughter, to pick up a piece of trash next to her foot.

The teenager turned up her nose and walked away!

What nerve!

She just blatantly ignored him!

What an attitude!

What disrespect!

My daughter, standing next to me, noticed this scene take place.

Knowing me and my tendencies to get stuck, she anticipated my next move and prompted me to **stop**.

"Ema?"

I looked at her and released a long breath I didn't notice I was holding.

I was **stuck on despair**.

That something like this could happen in the community in which I live.

I looked away and counted to 10.

I **thought** about how I feel that no young person should

show such disrespect to any authority figure.

Period!

And certainly not in my community.

I also thought about how I felt the need to confront this teenager right away and teach her a thing about respect.

Wait a minute. Do I need to?

Instead I **considered** I don't need to be everyone's parent.

There already was an adult on the scene and since I wasn't even part of the actual incident, I probably shouldn't stick my nose into it.

I got stuck on despair, but I'm **O.K.**

And I was grateful to be able to cradle my emotion in another point of view.

Stuck on: Why Did You Act Like That?

One Friday night after dinner, my family and I played a game of Ticket to Ride, a railway-themed board game.

Just as the game ended and my husband was preparing to tally up the points, my daughter announced she wanted her points tallied up first.

I knew she was convinced she had won.

And (so I thought), she wanted center stage.

"Why do you need to act like that?" I asked her. "Why can't

you just sit and wait patiently like everyone else?"

My words, intonation, and facial expressions were enough to silence her, then bring her to tears, ruining the good mood she was in.

She pushed her chair away from the table and ran to her room.

I knew I was stuck on wanting my daughter to act in a certain way. I deliberated, though. Was I really stuck? Is it really too much to expect that a 13-year-old girl act more graciously? Especially in front of her younger siblings?

I **closed my eyes** for a moment and took a deep breath.

I saw I was **stuck on disappointment** in my daughter.

I **uncovered** my beliefs. I realized how personally I took her reaction; as if her behavior reflected my parenting successes or failures.

But in thinking about that for a moment, I questioned myself. Does my daughter's every action reflect my parenting? I knew the answer was *no*.

I went to her room to process out loud the rest of my beliefs with her.

I found her on her bed, whimpering and hugging a pillow.

I sat down next to her and told her I was sorry.

I told her I got stuck on disappointment.

And that I reacted automatically based on my beliefs that my children should win gracefully.

And that, as the oldest, she should be a role model for her younger brothers. I admitted to her that I have very high expectations for her; that I do expect her to be perfect a lot of the time.

I also shared my fear of what her behavior may mean regarding my parenting.

I was embarrassed to admit these beliefs to my daughter.

(Well, at least the one about expecting her to be perfect.)

I told her I understood now she was just having fun, and that I was being insensitive in judging her and embarrassing her in front of everyone else.

I also told her I feel lucky she is my daughter.

I apologized, acknowledged I was wrong, and explained to her I had no intent to hurt her.

I acknowledged that I did, in fact, hurt her.

She gave me a big hug and through her sniffles said, "It's okay, Mom. You're actually a great mom. Thank you for processing this through with me. You're the best."

Which of course, brought me to tears, as well as to a place of **compassion** for myself and deep gratitude for this practice. Not to mention a renewed awareness of how mature my 13-year-old actually is.

Stuck on: Why Did I Listen to Her?

I was invited to a musical circle for "love and peace" a few months ago.

These events occur many times during the year across Israel in an effort to bridge the gaps between the Jews, Muslims, and Christians living in Israel.

I hadn't yet attended one of these circles.

But I heard they were wonderful.

Powerful.

People of all faiths gather to sing songs of peace.

Together.

In love.

And in hope.

Which I'm all for.

And I love singing. (In fact, my name, *Shira,* means music.) But when I called my friend up and invited her to join me at this event, she responded with, "You're honestly not going to that 'love and peace' circle, are you? You *know* what you're supporting when you go to those circles, right?"

"Huh?" I responded.

"You know. Left-wingers. They sing about 'love and peace', but they are so naive. It's gatherings like these that lead to giving up more Israeli land! And it is gatherings like these that will make Israel ultimately disappear one of these days.

It's a domino effect. Don't you see?"

"Are you kidding? That's not what this is about," I responded. "This has nothing to do with politics!"

"Oh, yeah? So, go. See for yourself."

I got off the phone hurt and disenchanted.

Her negativity left a bitter taste in my mouth.

Who the heck does she think she is?

But then I thought about what she said.

Is she right?

Maybe these events are all about naïve left-wingers dreaming impossible dreams.

Maybe I shouldn't go.

Maybe I don't belong in that kind of crowd.

I decided not to go.

I was content with my decision until the next morning, when I received a call from another friend who attended the event.

"It was amazing! I stayed until the end! It was just what I needed!"

I hung up the phone with her full of regret.

Feeling emotional, I **unrolled my yoga mat** and lay on my back.

I thought about how I was so **stuck on regret**.

I was *dissuaded by my friend's negativity.*

I **believed** in her beliefs and was persuaded.

Why do I let others do that to me?

And why is she so negative all the time?

Why is she so rude and obnoxious in sharing her harsh and antagonistic opinions with me?

I looked at my belief about my friend having no heart and about me always being weak.

But upon reflection, I acknowledged my friend *has* a heart.

And at the time of this incident, we were in the middle of a wave of terror attacks across the nation, and everyone was feeling on edge, including me.

I'm not always weak.

In fact, most of the time I stand my ground with my life choices.

And regarding my friend, she's actually got a huge heart.

She just has different beliefs than I do.

Maybe she was fearful and just wanted to warn me?

Maybe she thought she was trying to enlighten me. (She's a longtime Israeli and I didn't grow up here.)

I **considered** that I could have (and probably should have) gone to the event, despite my friend's opinions. I was hurt by my friend, but it was my choice, ultimately, not to go to the event.

I **consoled** myself, by remembering this wasn't the first 'love circle' to take place in Israel, and it won't be the last.

One day I'll participate in one, despite the fear and anxiety that may exist around me.

Stuck on: Why Can't You Climb the Wall?

My 7-year-old chose wall climbing as his after-school activity this year.

Each week, I drive him to his class and watch him climb.

If you can call it that.

Because he doesn't really climb.

Well, he does.

But he doesn't.

He gets all geared up, finds a partner, and *starts* to climb up the wall.

But he stops midway and calls to get down.

I wasn't concerned at first.

This is his first time wall climbing.

He's unfamiliar.

Give him time.

I noticed his teacher encouraging him to take one more step, reach for one more grip.

However, he would just hang on to the wall halfway up and wait until someone released him to get down.

This went on and on.

Week after week.

With no change.

I became frustrated at seeing him hanging, seemingly helpless, while all the other kids went up and down effortlessly.

So I intervened.

"You can do it. Just reach for one more with your left hand. Now try your right foot."

But after several sessions with several attempts of encouragement, I found my patience lessening because there was no progress.

I wanted him to get to the top!

I figured *he* wanted to get to the top!

I believed getting to the top was going to make him happy.

And me as well!

"Why am I paying for you to be in this class if you're not going to climb to the top?" I asked.

"Maybe this class isn't for you?" I called up to him.

I was rude.

I was unsupportive.

I was wrong.

I shouldn't have said those words, I realize now, but I did because at the time I was feeling something.

Feeling tightness in my neck, for one. I rubbed it and then **walked away** for several minutes and took some deep breaths trying to notice what I was stuck on.

It took a few minutes, but I realized I was **stuck on disappointment**.

I thought about it and then reflected upon my **beliefs**.

This class isn't for him? In other words, it's only for kids who already know how to climb to the top with ease? Really, Shira?

I **considered** that this struggle was, in fact, about me, and that my ego was getting in the way!

I considered getting to the top wasn't going to prove anything, nor was it going to help him much in his life if at all, and that I probably shouldn't care so much, especially if he's not making a big deal out of it, which he wasn't.

If he is happy coming to this class and happy with how he is climbing, that is all that matters.

I got stuck on disappointment, but I'm **O.K**. And so is he.

When my son came down, I apologized to him, gave him a big hug, and told him how proud I am of him.

And that he's doing great.

And that it doesn't really matter how high he climbs.

What matters most is that he's doing his best.

And having fun.

He smiled to me.

And proudly asked, "Did you see I got a little higher this time?"

Stuck on: Just Apologize Already!

My husband and I went on our weekly date night the other day.

We were invited to a *bat mitzvah* in Haifa, but with my daughter away for the summer, we couldn't find a babysitter to watch our three boys.

My husband asked me to contact his mom to see if she could help us out.

I was hesitant, because she's previously expressed how overworked she feels.

But I asked her anyway, and she agreed.

However, she requested that we bring the boys to her house instead of she coming to our house. This way, she wouldn't have to travel home late by herself.

When my husband and I dropped the kids off at her house

around 7 p.m., I told her we wouldn't be long. Three hours at most.

We thanked her again for babysitting and then drove to Haifa, a city half an hour away.

We were welcomed by the hosts and then mingled with the guests for quite some time.

Between the first few courses of delicious breads, dips, and salads, we enjoyed watching the young kids dance.

Around 9:30 p.m., our bellies full of delicious food, the DJ announced, "Come to the dance floor everyone, to burn off some calories before the main meal!"

Main meal?

After all this food?

There's more?

"Did he say main meal?" I asked my husband.

"Yup! Meat!" My husband replied with a smile.

Remembering the commitment I made to his mother, I suggested we say our thanks to the celebrating family and leave.

"We'll just skip the meal. No big deal," I said to my husband.

He disagreed.

He said it would be fine to stay a little longer.

That his mom wouldn't mind.

He was hungry, he said.

Hungry?

You're not hungry!

You just want to eat free food!

What about your mother?

Fifteen minutes later, the main meal still wasn't served, and I was getting antsy.

I reminded him of my concern.

At 10 p.m., I inquired rather gruffly, "It's kind of ridiculous that we're waiting around just to eat free food, don't you think?"

He let out a huge sigh and showed a face of defeat.

We said our goodbyes and headed out the door.

We rode home in silence.

By the time we got back to his mom's house at 11 p.m., we found her sitting outside on the porch, half asleep.

"Why are you out here?" my husband asked.

"Why?" she replied. "Because I had to wait up for you to pick up the kids!"

I knew it.

And I felt terrible.

My husband should apologize to her.

And then to me!

I was so right.

My husband was so wrong.

But I didn't say a word.

And neither did he.

We picked up our sleeping kids and transferred them into the car.

I sat in the passenger seat and stared out the window.

I was so angry.

The nerve!

I waited 10 minutes for him to say something.

Nothing.

What an ego he has!

But I knew I was stuck and didn't want to stay stuck.

So, I **stopped**.

I focused on some deep breathing.

I **told** myself I was stuck on anguish.

Uncovering my beliefs, I saw what was really bothering me: a belief that my husband's lack of respect towards his mom is recurring.

And that he owed her an apology, and that he was wrong to

not offer her one.

Yet thinking rationally, I acknowledged my husband has the utmost respect for his mother.

In fact, this was the first time an incident like this ever occurred, because the truth is, we hardly ever request his mother assist us with babysitting.

This situation was an anomaly.

And I **considered** maybe my husband, in an effort not to make the night longer than it already was, was planning to speak with his mom the next day.

And with that, I welcomed the silence on the car ride home.

I got stuck on anguish, wanting to have things go my way, and stuck on anger when they didn't, but I held myself in **compassion**.

It happens.

Stuck on: I'm a Terrible Mother

My daughter became a *bat mitzvah* not too long ago.

It was important to my husband and me that the focus of the *bat mitzvah* not be the party, but rather the religious service, and we conveyed this to our daughter.

The three of us brainstormed together and came up with a plan for a meaningful prayer service.

As for the part, we decided we'd invite her friends to the

community center for an alternative celebration to the traditional dance part and that I would run 12 different age-appropriate activities representative of each year of her life.

For instance:

Year 1 – The kids would sit on the floor and play with foam balls.

Year 2 – The kids would stand and spin in circles. Whoever remains standing last wins!

Year 3 – We would hand out bottles of bubbles.

Year 4 – They would participate in a balloon toss.

Year 5 – Each kid would create and color in a personal congratulations card to my daughter.

And so on and so forth, until age 12.

But as the proverb goes, "Man plans and God laughs."

And, oh boy, was God laughing at me that night.

The event actually started out beautifully, as the 50 or so kids watched an eight-minute video montage of my daughter's life.

The kids were calm, disciplined, and respectful.

I was relieved.

This is going to be a great evening!

And, my daughter is going to love me forever!

Then, I began to facilitate Year 1 which actually went well.

Until one of the boys stood up and started smacking another kid with a ball.

Oy!

The boys quickly got out of control.

Chaos!

And I got nervous.

All right, cut this activity short.

Next!

The kids, upon instruction, started spinning in circles (Year 2), but for some reason, I couldn't get the music going, and without the music, the atmosphere for that activity was lost.

Agh!

Keep going.

Year 3.

You can't go wrong with bubbles.

This activity went as planned.

But the boys couldn't handle Year 4.

Balloons.

While the girls blew up their balloons and tapped them back and forth to each other, the boys (unbeknownst to me) ran to the bathroom to fill theirs up with water.

Water bombs!

What a mess!

No! Have you no respect? Who's gonna clean this mess up?

As my husband took control of the situation, I continued on leading Years 5 and 6.

But when the kids started playing "Duck, Duck, Goose," one of the girls slipped on the spilled water from one of the water balloons and fell on her knee. She burst out in tears, partly from pain and partly from embarrassment.

This is going from bad to worse!

And with a break in flow of events, the kids started to lose focus.

The boys started running around.

The girls started taking out their cell phones.

Nothing was going as planned!

And I started to panic.

I still had another two hours to fill before the bus would come to take the kids home.

How did I let this happen?

I was in a panic, and so disappointed.

I knew my daughter was frustrated and embarrassed.

This party was a complete disaster.

There's no doubt I am the worst mother in the world.

I walked over to my daughter and nervously asked how she was doing.

She smiled and said she was fine.

She showed no sense of being upset or embarrassed.

She seemed genuinely happy.

It caused me to **stop**.

Really?

Could it be?

That this is all in my head?

I noticed I had been **stuck on guilt** just a few moments before **believing** I was the worst mother in the world.

"But what are we going to do for the next two hours?" I asked, afraid to hear her response.

But before she could answer, I noticed some of the girls crowding around the music player.

The same player that I couldn't successfully get to play music.

Suddenly, there was music blasting from the sound system.

From their smart phones.

Kids these days know everything!

All the kids started dancing!

Just like that.

I smiled to myself.

Hmm ... maybe I'm not the worst mother in the world?

Who needs to pay a DJ when you've got 12-year-olds who can run the show?

I dimmed the lights and the kids were in all their glory: dancing, jumping, hugging, giggling, and laughing.

At the end of the evening, the kids shouted out to me as they boarded the bus to go home:

"*Mazel tov!*"

"This was the *best* party ever!"

"We had so much fun!"

The best party ever?

Did I hear correctly?

You had so much fun?

For real?

I **considered** they were being honest.

When the last kid boarded the bus, my daughter gave me a great big hug and thanked me with complete sincerity.

The party was a success, even though I was certain it was a disaster.

Fortunately, I was able to come to another point of view and not get brought down by guilt. In doing this, I realized that everything was going to be **O.K.**—including me.

And, it was. Even better than **O.K.**

The party was unforgettable.

Stuck on: What Do I Do with All This Sugar?

Cakes.

Cookies.

Muffins.

Chocolates.

Hard candies.

Lollipops.

Marshmallows.

I guess you can say it kind of felt like Halloween around here.

But it wasn't.

It was the Jewish holiday of *Purim*.

During which there's a *mitzvah* (commandment of a good deed) to send gifts of food to at least one friend.

In our modern life, these gifts typically contain all kinds of pastries, including *hamantaschen*, traditional three-cornered Purim cookies.

My family, just like many families in my community, gives and receives many food packages during Purim.

Additionally, my kids participate in a food package swap with their classmates.

I can't stand the amount of sugar that suddenly appears in our house every year around this time.

I detest having all that junk in my house!

Sugar is poison!

I need to get that stuff out of my house as soon as it comes in!

Why do all holidays need to be centered around junk food?

This year, when my kids received their food baskets, I shared with them my feelings of agitation. "Into the trash the junk goes!" I said.

"Or give it away to your friends."

"But certainly do not keep it in this house!" I insisted.

"But they are *our* gift baskets, not yours!"

"We're allowed to keep what we received!"

"You're not being fair!"

Their cries caused me to **stop**.

I went over to the kitchen table and stared at all the gift baskets we received. I breathed in as I observed what sat in front of me. I tried to pinpoint the emotion I was feeling and where it was coming from. I was clearly averse to the packages, but why, really?

The packages were beautiful.

And colorful.

And plentiful.

I realized the deeper emotion I was feeling was **powerlessness**.

I uncovered my **beliefs** about having no control over what and how much my children consume during this holiday.

But thinking about that, I realized those beliefs weren't absolutely true.

It dawned on me, too, that I could use this as an opportunity to **consider** teaching my kids the concept of moderation.

And even start brainstorming ideas for unique healthy gift baskets for next year:

- Triangular-shaped mini-pizzas, instead of triangular-shaped cookies
- Vegetable sticks, instead of lollipops
- Cheese and olives, instead of hard candies and gummy worms

Maybe others would even catch on to this initiative!

But I chose not to get stuck on that expectation.

Instead, I reminded myself of this beautiful gift-giving commandment I became overcome with gratitude for all the gift baskets we received and for the people in our community who have become like family to us in the short amount of time we've lived here.

The sugar in our house is temporary.

It won't last.

I got stuck on powerlessness, but it was brief, and I'm **O.K.**

Next year, I will display my love and friendship to those in our community in innovative and healthful ways.

Because no one can overload on that.

Stuck on: How Did I Forget to Invite Guests?

I love *Sukkot.*

I was born on this holiday and so it holds a place of significance for me.

Plus, it arrives in fall, my favorite season.

The part I love most is the welcoming of guests into the *sukkah.*

Last week, I was quite busy preparing for the holiday.

I cooked, cleaned, decorated our *sukkah* with my kids, and cut down branches to lay across the top, close enough for shade, far enough apart to see the stars.

On the day of the eve of the holiday, it dawned on me that I was so busy with all the preparations that I totally forgot to invite guests for the first night!

Bummer!

How could I have forgotten something so simple?

In a last-minute attempt to invite guests, I called around to a few families, but it seemed that everyone already had plans.

What will my kids think?

They love having guests at our table more than I!

I was so disappointed in myself!

How could you be so mindless?

Inviting guests is such an integral aspect of the holiday!

This is going to ruin everything!

Besides inviting guests, everything else on the list was checked off.

The food was prepared.

The house was cleaned.

The *sukkah* was built and decorated.

Except for the roof.

We had it. We just hadn't attached it to the top of the *sukkah*.

I was in a bad mood as I threw branch after branch up to my husband, who was standing on top of our *sukkah,* waiting to retrieve them from me and attach them.

I made such a sour face as I was reprimanding myself.

See what multitasking does?

You need to be more mindful!

My 2-year-old was watching the scene, but he didn't understand why my husband was standing on top of the *sukkah*.

So he asked, *"Abba,* what are you doing?"

And, my husband wittily responded, "Making *Ema* happy."

I looked up at my husband.

And smiled.

Then laughed.

Because those three words **broke my moments of being stuck**.

I noticed how I was **stuck on guilt** among other things.

I thought about my **belief** that by not inviting guests I was going to ruin the entire holiday.

The entire holiday? I don't think so.

I **considered**:

So what if you have no guests tonight?

The holiday lasts seven days!

That means, seven breakfast opportunities to invite guests!

Seven lunches!

Six more dinners!

Endless opportunities to invite guests over for snacks!

It's the "time-for-happiness" holiday, for goodness' sake!

Look what you have in front of you:

A beautiful family!

A wonderful husband.

A warm community.

A gorgeous view.

Israel!

I got stuck on guilt, but I was **O.K**.

When my family sat in our *sukkah* that night, I smiled out of gratitude for my family and for our *sukkah,* which was imbued with love, compassion, and gratitude.

Open Workbook Pages – Stuck on Gloom

Can you think of a time you were stuck on gloom or any other emotion related to gloom as such as: disappointment, guilt, powerlessness, regret, shame? Use this page to reflect back on it or use this page the next time you get stuck. I urge you to take the opportunity to be vulnerable, identify the emotions they feel, and process through them.

Try to relive that story and complete the worksheet below to process through the experience. What or who triggered you? What happened?

_____

_____

_____

_____

_____

_____

_____

_____

_____

_____

S. **Stop**. After reading this short paragraph, close your eyes and visualize your "stuck" story. Imagine yourself taking a stop in that moment. Take some slow deep breaths and practice that stop here and now.

T. **Tell**. What does getting stuck on gloom feel like? Can you feel that emotion in your body? Scan your body and identify the spot where you felt it or still feel it. What does it feel like? A slight droop in your cheeks? Tired eyes? Tight jaw? Notice that feeling. Write it down.

U. **Uncover**. What are your beliefs in this particular story? Watch for words such as: "should have", "always", "never", or other ways of describing how things are "supposed" to be. Reflect on your beliefs and check the accuracy of each of them. Write them down.

C. **Consider**. What can you consider now regarding the story? What consideration did you or can you "take on?" Write it down.

_____

_____

_____

_____

_____

_____

_____

_____

K. **O.K.** Find compassion for yourself and remind yourself that it's O.K. to get stuck on something. Write yourself a note of forgiveness below.

_____

_____

_____

_____

_____

_____

_____

_____

Chapter 6: DESIRE

Stuck on: A Double Whammy!

In the past few years, I filled each day of winter vacation with some sort of fun, family-packed event for my kids, such as hikes, museums, and festivals. In Israel, we're lucky that the weather permits this.

But this year, with a rise in terrorist attacks and a recent near-deadly car accident, I preferred to keep a low profile for the week of break.

In fact, I preferred not to leave the house at all.

I just wanted to stay at home and work on writing this book.

So we didn't go anywhere.

On the first day of vacation, my boys jumped out of bed at dawn and screamed, "No school! Yippee!"

They danced around the living room in their pajamas.

After a few more hurrahs and a quick breakfast, the kids asked, "So, what are we doing today?"

"Uh, nothing?" I responded.

"Why?" they quickly retorted.

"Well, because," I stammered. "We have no plans for this vacation."

"So what are we supposed to *do*?"

"I don't know," I grumbled. "Find something to do. Play a game. Clean your room. Practice your guitar. Go for a walk."

They stood there with puzzled looks.

Apparently, those were not good ideas.

But, they had a good one!

Wrestle!

While they rolled around, I turned on the computer and started compiling the blog posts that would go under the chapter in this book, "Stuck on Desire."

But, the wrestling only lasted for about 10 minutes because one of the kids got hit in the head.

"It was his fault!" one said.

"But, he started!" the other griped.

"Now what can we do?" they both whined.

"We're bored!" they moaned.

Losing my patience, I offered, "Go to the basketball court."

"But no one is there!"

"*Everyone* is on vacation!"

"Yeah! Everyone except *us!*"

Guilt trip.

"Can we go on the computer?"

"No! You cannot go on the computer at 8 a.m. GO. FIND. SOMETHING. TO. DO!"

I returned to writing, and my kids put sock and shoes on and walked up to the basketball court.

Now, what was I thinking about a minute ago?

Darn.

I lost it.

And it was such a good thought!

Agh.

I just want to write!

My kids soon returned and resumed their screaming and whining.

I found myself going in and out of the kitchen.

For a handful of this and a handful of that.

A *latke* here.

A doughnut there.

I guess I was hungry.

Why am I so hungry?

Am I really hungry?

I noticed how my belly did not feel empty. Quite the contrary, I felt bloated. It was then I realized I was not hungry at all. I was simply stuck on a desire to eat.

But was there something more beneath that desire?

The morning passed and in the afternoon when the kids sat down for computer time, I **went to my bedroom**, lay on my yoga mat, and focused on my breath.

Inhale... Exhale...

Inhale... Exhale...

The thought of, "Get off this mat, Shira, and go downstairs for some hot chocolate" came to mind a few times.

Inhale, Exhale.

I put my hands on my bloated belly.

I still wasn't hungry. And I probably hadn't been hungry when I ate earlier.

All those times I kept returning to the kitchen for more food weren't out of true hunger.

I was eating to mask another emotion I wasn't prepared to truly feel.

It dawned on me that I was eating out of my unsatisfied **desire for wanting to work**.

Inhale... Exhale...

I checked in with my body and noticed my furrowed eyebrows, and released them.

I **thought** about the concept of *needing* to work on this book, and how having my kids at home was resulting in less time for me to work.

Inhale, Exhale.

Do I really need to work on this book today? Can it wait?

I **considered** that while my book can wait, my kids can't.

They'll bother me a whole lot less if I engage with them.

And when I engage with them, I do often have fun.

After a few more breaths, I got up from my mat and reunited with my kids.

"Who wants to go wall climbing?" I asked.

"Me! Me! Me! Me!" they cried.

I got stuck on desire (twice!), but it turned out **O.K.**

I was able to see past both the desires, return to some mindful eating, and savor the rest of the vacation with my children.

Stuck on: I Want to Give You Some Advice!

I wanted to give my friend some advice, even though he hadn't asked for it.

I wanted to pick up the phone and just tell him what was on my mind.

Something I think could help him out a bit.

I really, really wanted to tell him my thoughts.

My perspective.

After all, if someone else had thoughts they wanted to share with me, I would certainly be all ears.

So, why wouldn't he?

My opinions are of value.

I started to ponder how and when I would say what I wanted to say.

In fact, I obsessed over it.

I was thinking about it so much I couldn't concentrate on other things.

Noticing I was stuck, I **stopped** and closed my eyes.

Based on all my feelings of *wanting,* I could tell I was **stuck on desire**.

I scrutinized my **beliefs.**

Is my advice really valuable? How do I know that?

Would I honestly be open to hearing such unsolicited advice from others?

I **considered** what impact, if any, my advice would have on my friend's life once I shared my opinions with him.

And I considered that even with my children, I am very cautious about giving unsolicited advice.

I am not my friend's parent.

Perhaps I should keep my mouth closed.

Which is exactly what I did.

My friend was not in any danger, and my opinions, while worthy, may not have served any purpose other than to satisfy my desire to share them.

I got stuck on desire and it's **O.K.**

Processing through it helped me put me in my place.

Stuck on: You're Not Helping the Situation!

I work part-time as a research assistant for a company that creates and administers online surveys, prepares reports, and presents and conducts data analysis for nonprofit organizations.

One of my roles in the company is to program the online surveys into the system.

If the survey is straightforward, it doesn't require too much thinking on my end.

But sometimes, it can get complicated.

If respondent answers "Yes" to Question 2, then he should skip to Question 4.

If respondent answers "Yes" to Question 2 and "No" to Question 4, then he shouldn't see Page 5.

If respondent answers to being a teacher, he should not see Question 25.

But if respondent answers to being a teacher and he answers that he works in a private school, then he *should* see Question 25.

As the logical person that I am, I actually enjoy and feel challenged by some of these algorithms.

To me, they are fun!

Until they don't work.

At which point, it can turn into one big headache.

One day, I was programming one of those challenging surveys.

I felt under pressure to get my work done and have the survey ready to send out by my deadline.

But Question 16 wasn't working.

I checked my programming a thousand times.

I had the logic set up right.

What was going on?

I wrote an email to customer support, and within minutes they phoned me back.

The man who called sounded genuinely happy to help me resolve the issue.

"Let me just take a look. Give me a minute," he said.

"Sure," I responded gratefully.

After a minute, he told me he fixed the problem.

I checked, but it still wasn't working.

"Nope. Still not working," I said.

"Oh. Give me another minute."

I hung on, but I started to worry.

"Ok. Now try it," he said after three minutes.

I checked, but it still was not working.

What is going on here?

Does he not know what he's doing?

"Let me call you back, O.K.?" he asked.

Fine.

Call me back.

Just fix the problem!

And get back to me when it's fixed, will you?

I tried to remain patient, but felt myself getting more upset.

I found myself grunting and calling this guy names.

He called back five minutes later.

He told me he got it.

Except, he didn't.

Not only was Question 16 not working, the rest of the logic on that page was also messed up!

Four other questions were not working as programmed!

AGH!!!!!!!

"WHAT. DID. YOU. DO??????"

"YOU. MESSED. UP. ALL. MY. WORK!!!!" I said.

He told me he was going to ask his supervisor for help, and that he'd call me back when the issue was resolved.

I felt the annoyance in my heated face and heard the sounds of my huffing and puffing.

I knew I needed to **step away from my desk** and take some deep breaths.

I noticed stress in my forehead.

I acknowledged I was **stuck on frustration**.

I thought about how I **believed** this guy was not experienced enough to handle my case, and that this problem really shouldn't be so complicated to fix.

Is he not experienced? Do I really know that?

While I paced around for a few more minutes, I **considered** that this man was doing his best to help me, not hurt me.

I also considered that he probably had more experience than I was giving him credit for and that within five minutes, he'd probably resolve the issue.

He called back two minutes later saying he thought he finally fixed it.

I checked.

He did.

I knew he would!

I thanked him for his patience.

And he thanked me for mine.

I was able to move on with my work with a sense of **compassion** for myself and gratitude for the support I received.

Stuck on: I'm Trying to Meditate!

As a mother of four, I find that the early morning is the sweetest and most precious time of my day.

Nothing compares to it.

Especially at 5:30 a.m.

When it is quiet.

Because everyone is still asleep.

It's peaceful.

And it's my time for my spiritual practices.

My time to do yoga.

Or meditate.

Or pray.

Or a little of all three.

A few mornings ago, I did some yoga.

As I rolled out the mat and started with a few gentle poses, I noticed how wonderful it felt to stretch my body after a good night's rest.

But, then I heard a cry from one of the bedrooms.

"I'm going to throw up!"

Agh.

Great.

After a five minute episode in the bathroom, I finally accompanied my son to the living room, covered him with blankets on the couch, and told him to rest.

He watched me practice.

Fine. No big deal.

It could be worse.

I continued with my poses.

Fifteen minutes later, another child got out of bed.

He grabbed a mat and placed it right next to me.

I gave him a look. "What? I can't do yoga with you?" he asked.

Huh?

I started to feel frustrated.

This is my time!

My quiet spiritual practice time!

That I'm supposed to be doing alone!

Agh.

Fine. No big deal.

I reminded myself to come back to my center.

And find my peace.

But soon, another child got out of bed and said he wanted to meditate.

He rolled out a yoga mat on the other side of me, sat Buddha-style, placed his hands on his knees with his palms up and chanted:

"Ohmmmm ..."

I stared at him.

Is this kid for real?

None of you are supposed to even be awake!

Why can't I practice my yoga without being interrupted by little people?

Have you no respect at all for me?

But, when I heard my inner voice and felt my jaw tense, I realized I didn't like what I heard or what I felt.

I **stopped** and closed my eyes and took several deep breaths.

I knew I was **stuck on frustration**.

I noticed my belly was all tangled up in knots.

I breathed into that area of my body and started to notice my belly muscles relaxing.

I **uncovered** my beliefs about "my time" and how this situation wasn't "fair" and it would ruin my morning.

I thought about how I deserve "my" time.

But upon reflection, I recognized I do get a lot of "my" time.

A lot.

Nearly every morning.

And that this unusual situation did not have to ruin my day.

In that moment, I **considered** that I did get a bit of yoga practice in already (even though it wasn't as long as I wanted) and for that I should be grateful.

I got stuck on frustration, but I **held myself in compassion**.

At that moment, I looked at the clock.

6:50 a.m.

Something was supposed to happen at 7 a.m.

What was it?

Think. Think!

Oh, the Times Square ball drop!

It's a new year!

I told the kids and got them excited.

I rushed to turn on the laptop and raced to find a live stream video of the event.

At that point, the entire family was awake and we all gathered around to watch the celebration in New York City.

As I took a step back and looked at my family, I reminded myself of how lucky I am.

For my husband.

And my children, some of whom are even interested in yoga or meditation.

How cool is that?

And that having these children in my life actually enhances my life.

Actually, my children are my practice.

A life practice.

And with that revelation, I welcomed in a new year.

Stuck on: I Want What You Have!

One Shabbat evening this year, friends in our community (who also immigrated from the United States) celebrated their son's *bar mitzvah*. As I entered the synagogue for prayers that Friday night, I was overcome with joy and happiness for them.

The faces of the grand-parents, siblings, uncles, aunts, and cousins, all of whom had flown in from abroad for the occasion, showed such happiness.

How lucky is this bar mitzvah boy! To be surrounded by so much love! So much family!

And, then it hit me. A nervous thought.

What about my family?

We're the next family in line in our community to celebrate a bat mitzvah!

And that's when my heart skipped a beat.

What if none of my family comes?

Is my daughter going to blame me for having left America in the first place?

What if the synagogue will be completely empty?

I want a packed synagogue exactly like tonight!

Noticing lots of emotions arise in me, I suddenly felt a surge of positive energy as my friends and neighbors began to sing in praise.

I **focused on the expression of their faces** and their joyous prayers.

And then I **told** myself I was stuck on jealousy.

I **thought** about how I believe *their* child is lucky, and *their* child is surrounded by love, but *my* child was going to be disappointed and blame me.

But upon reflection on those beliefs, I realized they were unfounded.

I **considered** the ways in which our celebration was going to be meaningful and beautiful, no matter what.

Even if my family from abroad couldn't be there.

I even visualized the day itself—with my daughter standing at the Torah, reading. I could already feel growing excitement.

My jealousy didn't completely disappear, nor did my feelings of guilt, but I was able to see a different perspective and move past it in that moment.

In my visualizations, I saw my friends and neighbors in the room. I pictured particular families we're close with. I imagined my husband's Israeli family in the room, too. I realized, in fact, the synagogue will be filled.

And while I also acknowledged my community can never replace my own extended family, I recognized the huge role it does play in our current lives.

And that without my community, I would really feel the sense of being alone in a foreign country.

And for that, I reminded myself I was **O.K.**

Even more than O.K.—I was blessed.

Open Workbook Pages – Stuck on Desire

Can you think of a time that you were stuck on desire or another emotion related to desire such as: frustration or jealousy? Use this page to reflect back on it or use this page the next time you get stuck on any of those emotions. I urge you to take the opportunity to be vulnerable, identify the emotions they feel, and process through them.

Try to relive that story and complete the worksheet below to process through the experience. What or who triggered you? What happened?

_____

_____

_____

_____

_____

_____

_____

_____

_____

_____

_____

S. **Stop**. After reading this short paragraph, close your eyes and visualize your "stuck" story. Imagine yourself taking a stop in that moment. Take some slow deep breaths and practice that stop here and now.

T. **Tell**. What does desire feel like? Can you feel that emotion in your body? Scan your body and identify the spot where you feel it. What does it feel like? Tightness? Ache? Burning? Notice that feeling. Write it down.

U. **Uncover**. What are your beliefs in this particular story? Watch for words such as: "should have", "always", "never", or other ways of describing how things are "supposed" to be. Reflect on your beliefs and check the accuracy of each of them. Write them down.

C. **Consider**. What can you consider now regarding the story? What consideration can you "take on?" Write it down.

K. **O.K.** Find compassion for yourself and remind yourself that it's O.K. to get stuck on something. What kind words would you say to a friend who got stuck? Write that to yourself below.

Chapter 7: JOY

Stuck on: I Want to Bring Lots of Gifts

For the past six years, on every trip back to the United States to visit my family, I bring gifts for my family and friends.

Over the years, I've brought back new Israeli wines, handmade jewelry, soaps and olive oil from the Galilee, Bedouin teakettles, handmade *challah* boards, local spices, chocolates, *halvah*, teas and coffees, and Dead Sea soaps and creams.

Why do I do this?

Partly because I want to support the local businesses here.

Partly because I want to express my pride in Israel and share that with others.

And partly because I am generous.

And I like being generous.

This year, I picked up a new hobby.

Painting.

I decided that instead of purchasing gifts this year, I would bring my family and friends handmade artwork.

So I went to the local art store.

Purchased canvases, paintbrushes, and acrylic paints, and started to paint.

The problem was, having little to no experience with painting, my artwork didn't turn out well.

But I really wanted to bring back some beautiful homemade gifts. Nothing was going to stop me.

So, I watched a movie clip on YouTube to learn calligraphy in order to paint the Hebrew letters on the new canvases I bought so that the letters would appear as if they just jumped out of a Torah scroll.

Not easy, but, I was on a mission.

The outcome?

Completely amateur and certainly not like what you see at the famous artist colony of *Tzfat* (which is what I was striving for).

Feeling directionless and stuck on needing to bring gifts with me, I **stopped.**

I **told** myself I was stuck on generosity.

And closed my eyes and **thought** about how all of my friends and family are expecting me to bring them gifts every year.

Wait a minute. Are they really expecting this from me?

And I thought about my belief that if I don't bring everyone gifts, my friends will regard me as selfish and uncaring.

Really, Shira?

And then I **considered** something completely unreasonable.

I considered *not* bringing gifts this year.

And that no one would be disappointed in me.

In fact, I **considered** everyone would be fine if I showed up without gifts.

So, I left the paints and canvases behind for the kids.

And got on the plane empty-handed.

But full of heart and full of **compassion**.

Considering that we, my family and I, could be the gifts this year.

Stuck on: I Can't Wait to See My Family!

On the plane ride to the United States, I became excited.

I always do.

We only get to see my family once a year.

So I really look forward to this time to be with everyone.

My parents generously open their house for us to stay.

For three weeks.

And along with my sister, brother and their families, we take all the kids to fun destinations like: Sesame Place, Hershey Park, and Ocean City, NJ!

I get to see one of my grandmothers, (my other one lives in Florida), and meet up with dozens of aunts and uncles and cousins and friends.

I show my kids where I went to high school and share many childhood memories with them.

I love these trips.

Which is why I thought this trip would be awesome.

The problem was, I didn't consider that while family vacations can be awesome, they are not a 24/7 lovefest.

And I forgot that family vacations can be hard work.

Like, for instance, managing my youngest children who wake up at the crack of dawn because they are hungry and want breakfast!

They don't necessarily grasp that their grandparents are still sleeping at that hour.

And that their grandparents can hear every single whisper the kids make.

Every morning I found myself first whispering, then quietly yelling, "Shh!" until my parents woke up.

It wasn't easy.

In fact, it was stressful.

Also, we don't keep our house as tidy as my parents do, but my parents expect us to maintain the standards of their house, and so, that can be stressful on me and my parents as well.

While we're there, I do my best to be on top of everyone.

Even on top of my husband, who tends to be lax about such

things.

But I'm not perfect.

Stuck on anticipation, I forgot about all these other thoughts.

I didn't foresee any conflicts.

I believed all would be fine and dandy.

Because that's how vacations are supposed to be.

Until they go sour.

At which point, I just want to go back home.

My home.

The one I live in and manage now.

Not the one I grew up in, and in which I have to live up to someone else's standards, and where everyone loses their patience for one another.

And I just want to abandon ever agreeing to these family visits again, because they are just too difficult and too stressful.

But in the midst of some challenging family vacation moments this time, I caught myself with these negative, despairing thoughts, and forced myself to **stop**.

I closed my eyes.

I took a deep breath.

And reminded myself how I was **stuck on anticipation,** not just for the fine and dandy moments, but also for the inevitable disasters!

Which led me to question my original belief that everything will be hunky-dory on family vacations.

Is there such a thing as a perfect family? A stress-free vacation with small children?

And then, I **considered** how darn lucky I am that my parents are alive.

And healthy.

And enjoy engaging so much with my children.

And make time for us when we come in for our yearly visits.

And feed us.

And pamper us.

And take my kids out to the movie theater, miniature golfing, and to restaurants.

I considered how fortunate we are to be healthy enough to make these visits and that my parents welcome us graciously into their home each summer even though things have gone sour in the past.

And that while wonderful in so many ways, no family visits can be 100% perfect all of the time.

And really none of our small conflicts are things that can't be worked out. They can and always do.

I got stuck on anticipation, but **it's all right.**

If I didn't love my family, I wouldn't be excited to visit them in the first place.

Stuck on *S.T.U.C.K.*

Last fall, I had an experience of a lifetime: a mother-daughter bonding opportunity trip to Eilat.

Just the two of us.

My daughter had been dreaming about swimming with the dolphins.

And now I was going to give her the opportunity to make that dream come true.

We were both excited to get away.

We had just been in a near-death car accident a few days before.

I tried to leave behind the lingering tension and pain in my head and shoulders.

I allowed my daughter to plan the long weekend away.

We went snorkeling for the first time.

My daughter went parasailing.

I got a fish pedicure.

And my daughter bought new shoes.

And of course, she swam with the dolphins.

Whatever she wanted to do, I arranged.

But although I was with her physically 100%, I can't say I was with her mentally all of the time.

In addition to the lingering pain I was experiencing, my attention was being drawn to writing this book.

I had just finished the first draft and was already dreaming about life after the book.

So while my daughter was swimming with the dolphins, my mind was swimming with ideas for a Getting *un*STUCK workbook companion, bumper stickers, and key chains!

And while I was snorkeling with my daughter, I was dreaming of giving workshops on cruises instead of being in complete awe of the extravagant colors and coral right in front of my eyes.

The future is going to be amazing!

The ideas continued to rush to my mind, and I continued to chase after them.

Until I heard my daughter call out: "Ema? Did you hear what I just said?"

I had been daydreaming.

Nope. I totally missed what you just said.

Sheesh. What kind of mother am I?

Remembering I wanted to give my daughter the undivided attention she deserved and that I promised her, I **stopped** and took a breath.

I told her I was **stuck on excitement**.

And that I **believed** all of those thoughts regarding the future of The S.T.U.C.K. Method to be real.

Am I just stuck on desire again?

I **considered** how being stuck on excitement was clouding my opportunity from just being present with my daughter.

And pulling me away from enjoying every moment with her.

I realized, among many other considerations, that whether Getting *un*STUCK grows into a best-selling book or not is not what mattered in that moment.

What mattered most was giving my attention to my daughter on this once-in-a-lifetime trip.

And that is exactly what I did.

And I was **O.K.**

Open Workbook Pages – Stuck on Joy

Can you think of a time you were stuck on joy or any other emotion related to joy such as: anticipation, excitement, or generosity? Use this page to reflect back on it or use this page the next time you get stuck on any of those emotions. I urge you to take the opportunity to be vulnerable, identify the emotions they feel, and process through them.

Try to relive that story and complete the worksheet below to process through the experience. What or who triggered you? What happened?

_____

_____

_____

_____

_____

_____

_____

_____

_____

_____

_____

S. **Stop**. After reading this short paragraph, close your eyes and visualize your "stuck" story. Imagine yourself taking a stop in that moment. Take some slow deep breaths and practice that stop here and now.

T. **Tell**. What does getting stuck on joy feel like? Can you feel that emotion in your body? Scan your body and identify the spot where you feel it? What does it feel like? Heart racing? Thirst? Hunger? Notice that feeling. Write it down.

U. **Uncover**. What are your beliefs in this particular story? Watch for words such as: "should", "always", "never", or other ways of describing how things are "supposed" to be? Reflect on your beliefs and check the accuracy of each of them. Write them down.

C. **Consider**. What can you consider now regarding the story? What consideration can you "take on?" Write it down.

_____

_____

_____

_____

_____

_____

_____

K. **O.K.** Find compassion for yourself and remind yourself that it's O.K. to get stuck on something. What kind words would you say to a friend who got stuck? Write that to yourself below.

_____

_____

_____

_____

_____

_____

_____

Part III: Embracing The S.T.U.C.K. Method

Why do we get stuck on things?

What prevents us from separating ourselves from our stories? What stops us from simply moving on after incidents that upset or frustrate us? Why does the process of getting unstuck require such effort?

These questions have occupied the minds of philosophers, psychologists, and spiritual leaders. My own answer is that human beings must be wired to stay attached to our one-sided stories and that getting stuck on things is simply human nature. In other words, getting stuck is inevitable.

We carry lots of emotions, and much of the time, we do so unconsciously. Invariably, we get stuck on them. The S.T.U.C.K. Method is about seeing opportunities and moving on. No matter which emotion you're stuck on, or how many layers it has, what matters most is that you recognize you are stuck on something and make an effort to process through it. It's about movement.

That's why remembering and applying The S.T.U.C.K. Method to our lives requires effort. In yoga and in mindfulness work, we often refer to this recurring pattern of working on ourselves and forgetting to work on ourselves as "practice." By practice, I mean our use of The S.T.U.C.K. Method is not a cure: instead, it is a tool that is meant to be used time and time again. We might get better at it, and then we might forget to use it, and then we remember again and implement it again, and so on. A practice.

You have learned the five steps of The S.T.U.C.K. Method—and I hope you can use all the various "muscles" that need to be strengthened in order to integrate this method into your life. Yes, you may be unsteady and unsure at first. There will be pitfalls, and you may find that some emotions are easier to process than others. And when, for instance, deeply rooted emotions are provoked, it may take extra time and energy for you to recognize them and to process through them. Even the first simple step of stopping is not so simple—it takes a lot of practice and willpower. Take, for instance, the following story, during which I found it very difficult to implement a stop.

Stuck on: Waze

Not long ago, my husband, children and I went on a family hike to a place we had never been.

As my husband pulled out of the parking lot of our community, I noticed he was plugging his phone into the car adapter and turning on the navigation app Waze.

"Do you want help with that? I'd be happy to navigate," I said.

"No, I'm good," my husband replied.

Sitting in the passenger seat while the driver's attention is partly on his phone really makes me anxious. I noticed my upset, but chose to ignore it.

We drove for 20 minutes when my husband picked up his phone again and looked at it.

"You know, it really makes me nervous when you use your phone while driving. Can you please let me hold the phone?" I asked.

"I do this all the time!" He was getting annoyed. "How do you think I get to my new job sites for work? I've got a perfect driving record! Just calm down!"

Agh.

I can't stand it when people tell me to calm down!

I closed my eyes.

I took a deep breath.

Ten minutes from our destination, he again glanced at his phone.

I began to shout. "Do I need to treat you like one of the kids? Do I really need to parent you? Driving while looking at your phone is dangerous! Don't you know most car accidents these days are caused because of cell phone usage? I will not stand for it in this car! Especially with the four children in it!"

Then, my husband also flipped out, yelling about how he's a safe driver and can handle doing two things at once and ...yadda, yadda, yadda.

I couldn't hear what he was saying.

I could only hear the story in my mind.

Because I was right.

100%.

There was no doubt about it.

None whatsoever.

The problem was, which I couldn't see at the time, being right never helps solve a problem when you are in the middle of it.

We continued to scream it out (yes, in front of our children) until my husband just yelled, "**Stop!**"

Does he know The S.T.U.C.K. Method?

And the car went silent.

No one said a word until the car was put into park.

Oh, I was **stuck on frustration**, you can be sure about that!

But at the same time with the silence surrounding us, I was able to center myself enough to process the incident and my **beliefs** around it. I thought about how my husband should have known better and should have respected my wishes. I thought about how he was entirely wrong.

Certain of my beliefs, I told myself I had nothing else to consider.

Nothing.

I was really, really stuck.

But knowing that many of our beliefs are not 100% accurate, I tried to and succeeded in uncovering one last belief.

I **believed** I *needed* to have that conversation in that moment.

Did I really? Could I have waited until we arrived at our destination, instead of bringing it up while he was driving?

I stretched my **consideration** muscles the best I could and finally came up with the following:

I *could* have waited to speak to him later that night when we were both calm and not in the heat of the moment and, in that conversation, request that I would be the driver on our family vacations from now on.

I got stuck on frustration, but it's **OK.**

Later, I apologized and we were able to move on from the incident. I still haven't decided if it's important enough to me that I always be the driver on our family vacations in order to avoid this from happening again in the future, but I plan to keep considering that.

∼

This story is nothing new. In fact, if you substitute "Waze" for "orange curtains," you have the same story as "Stuck on: We Need Some Orange Curtains!" (See page 13). Same concept, different scenes. I had my beliefs; he had his. We had a difference of opinion, which led to an eruption.

We continue to get stuck on things because triggers will never cease to exist. They will endure as long as we live and no matter how often we practice. Outer triggers such as unexpected traffic, no milk left in the refrigerator for your morning coffee, and the electricity suddenly going out are as common as inner-voice triggers like, "You're not good enough," "You're fat," or "You should feel guilty." All of us have at least one dominant, recurring trigger, too. Reflect on your life for a moment. What or who is your recurring trigger? Could it be your spouse? Your mother? Mother-in-law? Your boss? Your financial situation? Your weight? Be honest.

My recurring trigger is my husband. And this is not to say that I don't love my husband. Nor is it to say I don't admire or highly respect him. I do. I also know I trigger him, as well. My expectations of him are actually desires that lead to frustration when I feel as if he is not listening to me or does not see the world the way I see it. For many years, these recurring situations at home saddened me. Until one day while implementing The S.T.U.C.K. Method, it dawned on me that I could consider the incidents between my husband and me as a gift and that I could consider my triggers as my greatest opportunities for self-growth and development. It took me a while to understand this and appreciate it, but when I did, doing so turned my life around.

For example, my husband has an expectation of how I should do the dishes. I don't live up to that expectation and it triggers him. And when he gets triggered, I react and get stuck on resentment. Yet, with experience, I've learned to anticipate my dishwashing style will trigger my husband. Therefore, I can strategically put myself in a place of control and prepare for a stop. Additionally, when my husband is stuck on something, I often now recognize it as an opportunity to practice compassion and loving-kindness. Not always, but with each day, more and more often.

It is important to note that while others get stuck on things too, naming that doesn't often help in the midst of the situation. From my experience, attempting to enlighten my husband (or anyone else for that matter) is futile. If my husband is stuck on something, the last thing he wants is to listen to me preach The S.T.U.C.K Method to him. He is in his own story and he must decide how he will deal with the situation. He is the only one who has the power to get unstuck anyway. I cannot do that for him.

S.T.U.C.K. for Your Personal Growth

The S.T.U.C.K. Method is about looking at your *own* life and taking on the practice of transforming yourself and your relationships. It is empowering!

While you certainly can share this book with others and acknowledge the benefits this practice has brought to your life, using The S.T.U.C.K. Method is really all about *your* personal growth, and not changing any other person. Keep in mind that this practice is meant for *you* and is not about you trying to fix *other* people.

Sometimes two people may be stuck on something at the same time in the same story. In the next story, you will see that even though I noticed my husband was also stuck on something, and that all I wanted to do in that moment was place the blame on him, I eventually recognized I had an opportunity to practice. His "stuck" story was his own story. And my responsibility was to process through my own.

Stuck on: My Plan is Better!

Two days ago, my family and I set out for a vacation weekend to the Dead Sea.

Among many other activities, climbing Masada mountain was on our list of things to do.

On the Wednesday before departing, my husband asked me to pack up the family and prepare to be ready to go by 2 p.m. the next day.

This request was fine with me. I don't really mind packing up four of the six of us. (My husband and my oldest child pack their stuff on their own.)

Besides the mandatory things (clothes, bathroom items, and food), I made sure to pack four small backpacks, four hats, and four bottles of water for my little boys and me, because on our last family hike, we didn't bring enough water, one of my children got badly dehydrated, and I learned from that experience.

So, Thursday afternoon we drove down to the Dead Sea and stayed over at a youth hostel.

In the morning, as we were about to get in the car to head to the Masada National Park, I did a quick check.

Six hats?

Check.

Six backpacks?

Check.

Six bottles of water?

Nope.

Only four.

"Where are the other two?" I asked randomly.

"Who knows?" was the response I got from one of my kids.

Oy.

So I said to my husband, "Well, we'll just have to stop at a gas station and pick up two more bottles on the way."

He didn't agree.

He said four bottles would be enough.

But, in my mind, we each needed to carry our own.

We needed six bottles of water.

One for each of us.

I mean, really.

What's the big deal about picking up two more bottles of water?

Was he just trying to save a few shekels?

Was it a matter of principle? Like: I was the one who packed so I would have to deal with the consequences of not being fully prepared?

Something having to do with saving the environment?

I just didn't get it!

To me, we were talking about a health and security issue.

I insisted he explain to me why he was being so stubborn about this.

He explained that if we add up the total number of liters with the bottles we already had, it was enough water to cover the six of us for this hike.

"Yes, but we could also stop at the gas station on the 15 minute drive down to Masada and pick up two more bottles of water so that everyone can carry their own," I responded.

He didn't budge.

"Why are you being so stubborn?" I asked.

We bickered back and forth in front of the kids.

It was ugly.

And not such a great way to start the morning.

I knew I was stuck.

When one of my kids insisted from the backseat we go for marriage therapy already, I shut my mouth and rode in silence to our destination.

We arrived at Masada, still with only four water bottles.

As we started to climb the mountain, still not speaking to one another, I finally decided to start to process.

I **stopped** in my tracks, took in the gorgeous view of the Dead Sea, and breathed in deeply. I noticed physically I was holding my frustration between my eyebrows. As I continued to breathe and pay attention to that area of my body, I became aware of a physical relief.

I **told** myself that I was stuck on frustration that my husband was arguing with me instead of following my plan to ensure each family had a water bottle to carry.

I **believed** that everyone in my family should carry their own water bottles on hikes and that my husband always underestimates the importance of water!

I also thought about how my husband should always agree with me!

Reflecting on those beliefs, I know there weren't entirely accurate.

And I **considered** that my husband was right.

Maybe we did have enough water.

I **considered** that my husband is responsible and wouldn't do anything to put our family in harm.

And I can **considered** that I don't always have to be the sole decision maker in the family.

I chose to let go of my need for the situation to proceed as I planned, recognize that the four bottles would be fine this time, and coordinate our pre-trip planning more effectively next time.

I got stuck on frustration, and it's **O.K.**

I caught up with my husband and told him that I processed through what happened. I acknowledged the beliefs I held and the new considerations I came to. With that, he gave me a hug and thanked me, and we were able to continue our day with joy and ease.

∼

In the story above, I took on processing through The S.T.U.C.K. Method because I wanted to get out of that small, clenched-up, frustrated place. My choice of taking on a new viewpoint was not about giving in to my husband, nor was it necessarily about compromising. This was not about winning or losing a battle. Rather, it was about my interest in and commitment to ongoing self-growth, to healing, and to getting to a short-term resolution for what seemed like a dead-end argument. It was about feeling better in the moment. I took on a new perspective, not to appease him, but rather to acquire the freedom from being stuck on something in the first place.

Healing After Conflict, Preventing a Crisis

In the "Stuck on: My Plan is Better!" story, I implemented The S.T.U.C.K. Method only after the disagreement I had with my husband erupted. One of the great things about The S.T.U.C.K. Method is that it can be used as a healing measure after a conflict has already transpired or as a preventative measure to avoid potential conflicts.

As a healing measure, you may choose to apply The S.T.U.C.K. Method to reflect upon the events that led to the deadlock and seek healing from it. Once processed, it also empowers you to approach any other parties involved and share with them your previous mindset and your new frame of reference, thereby supporting opportunities for apologies and acceptances of them.

In the scenario above, I was able to recognize the most important aspect to the story was that my family had enough water for the hike. That's it. Though the chosen plan was not *my* plan, I was able to release my limited way of thinking about my family's safety and proceed with the day, not from a place of resentment, but rather from a place of contentment that I possessed the freedom to move on. I certainly did not want to spend the rest of my day fighting with or not speaking to my husband. I wanted to enjoy the hike and the day with my family, which is exactly what happened.

Over time and experience, you may catch yourself when you are stuck before a crisis erupts and be able to implement The S.T.U.C.K. Method as a preventative measure. You can begin to process through The S.T.U.C.K. Method and possibly avoid any inner or external conflicts that may otherwise ensue.

You do not need to tell other people when you are processing through The S.T.U.C.K. Method. It can be done privately and quietly. Below is an example of a story in which I used The S.T.U.C.K. Method as a preventative measure. I processed through the steps silently while sitting in a prayer service.

Stuck on: "Jingle Bells" in Synagogue?

One winter Friday night in the synagogue, the prayer leader for that evening service sang the pinnacle prayer of welcoming the Sabbath "Queen" (*L'cha Dodi*) to the tune of "Jingle Bells."

I was shocked.

Really?

Seriously?

Am I hearing correctly?

My daughter, sitting next to me, whispered to me, "Is this 'Jingle Bells'?"

"Yes," I answered. "If I were the prayer leader, I never would have done that!" I replied judgmentally. I was surprised, because I associate "Jingle Bells" with Christmas, with Christianity. Not with Judaism, nor with Jewish prayer on the Sabbath.

What should I do?

Should I walk out of the synagogue in protest?

Should I stay, but not sing along?

Should I say something to the prayer leader at the end of the service?

While I was losing my focus and concentration on the prayer itself and certainly stuck, I decided to process.

I **stopped**, closed my eyes, placed one hand on my belly and took a breath. I noticed my belly felt tight, but the more I breathed and focused on my belly, I noticed more of a release.

I thought about which emotion I was holding onto and **told** myself I was stuck on frustration and that a prayer leader had the audacity to sing a Christmas tune in our synagogue, and I had no ability to stop it.

I also felt stuck on righteousness.

I **uncovered** my beliefs.

I thought about how Christmas tunes should not be sung in a synagogue, and "Jingle Bells" is a Christmas tune and that because I live in Israel, I shouldn't have to be inundated with Christmas tunes during Christmas season.

I also thought about how the prayer leader doesn't ever consider other people's feelings.

After reflecting on those beliefs, I came up with a list of considerations because I realized my beliefs weren't entirely true.

I can **consider** that the prayer leader may have consulted with others before deciding to introduce this tune and that the prayer leader did not intentionally try to diminish the prayer service.

I **considered** that the prayer leader is a caring person and may have believed he was bringing great joy to the congregation with the use of this tune.

I **considered** that I am no better a person than the prayer leader and that instead of judging the prayer leader, I could focus on the words and be grateful for the opportunity to pray together with my community.

I chose to give the prayer leader the benefit of the doubt and rejoice in the prayer rather than allowing the tune to ruin my focus and concentration.

I got stuck on frustration and righteousness, but it's **O.K.**

When I focused my attention on my new perspective, I found myself in a heightened sense of concentration on the words of the prayer compared to how I probably typically am when in which I am probably less attuned to them.

~

Time: It's Part of the Process

Before I started to process through The S.T.U.C.K. Method in the above story, I felt I was *right* in my belief that "Jingle Bells" was an inappropriate tune to be sung in the synagogue. When you are stuck on something, you feel *right*. You believe that everyone else around you is *wrong*. At heart, this is because the emotion you are stuck on serves you in some way. In this case, believing that the prayer leader should not be singing a Christmas tune in the synagogue made me feel morally superior to him, and it protected me from feeling wrong. Yet while staying stuck can protect you, it doesn't promote any growth or healing.

Processing through The S.T.U.C.K. Method can take as little as one minute (as with "Jingle Bells") or it can take much longer, depending on the size of the obstacle you are facing. Additionally, even when you successfully move through and implement The S.T.U.C.K. Method, your emotions still may linger. Yet even strong emotions tend to dissipate with time, though some emotions may last longer than others. In the meantime, while these emotions still endure, you can consider speaking to a friend who practices The S.T.U.C.K. Method, as well as continue to cradle your emotion in another point of view.

Indeed, sometimes you need time before you are ready to process through The S.T.U.C.K. Method at all. You may feel so deeply attached to your beliefs that considering other options seems entirely impossible. Be patient with yourself. I've been there, too. Once, for instance, it took several weeks before I was ready to process entirely through The S.T.U.C.K. Method; the **C** step was a challenge for me.

Stuck on: Fear in the Middle East

I've been sitting with this for a while.

For lots of reasons.

Fear.

Paranoia.

Concern that by admitting my fear I'd be raising the anxiety of others.

Especially that of my family members who live far away.

Or friends that are debating coming to Israel for a visit.

But here I am.

Finally writing about it.

A couple of weeks ago, I admitted to my closest friend here that I am afraid.

Her response?

"Shira, if you're afraid, we're all in trouble."

I didn't specify afraid of what exactly.

But she knew.

Otherwise, she would have asked.

It's not necessarily the political situation here in Israel—because the political situation is the political situation, and that hasn't changed since the declaration of this country's independence 67 years ago.

Anti-Semitism.

Anti-Zionism.

It has been in existence all these years.

Everyone knows that.

But what has changed, at least in the last month, are the methods of terrorism.

Whereas in the past, there have been (and will continue to be) suicide bombers whose aim is to blow up as many innocent civilians in one shot as possible, now it has become less planned, more random, more heinous.

Using random household tools:

Axes.

Screwdrivers.

Kitchen knives.

You can be anywhere, anywhere—a shopping mall, a bus stop, or just walking down the street—and the worst nightmare that you have ever considered could come your way.

And, if that's not enough to make you afraid, then take a look at the age of some of the recent terrorists.

13.

13!

And if that's not enough, what about the demonstrations that took place down the street from our *kibbutz*?

A place that would take me about a two minutes' walk to get to.

Just at the entrance of the local Arab village, whose population is 15 times that of my community.

And we're not talking about peaceful demonstrations.

We are talking here about angry, rock-throwing, very loud demonstrators.

Who are throwing rocks at cars passing by.

At my friends who are simply going to work!

Paranoia set in.

And when I considered what exactly it was I was afraid of, I realized (if it's not obvious), that I was afraid for my own life.

I was afraid that perhaps I would be the next victim of the next random act of terrorism.

I was afraid that perhaps the otherwise nice Arab lady who sells me cheese every week at the supermarket would one day decide to use her knife for other purposes.

I was afraid that the friendly Arab man who frames the houses in my husband's construction business and didn't show up to work last week because he was striking, along with all the other Arabs across the country, may decide to use his tools for something other than framing homes.

I was afraid what my kids' Arab bus driver could do.

I don't even want to think what the Arab orthodontist, who is supposed to start treating my daughter next week, could do out of temporary insanity or anger.

I was afraid because I don't feel prepared for any of these situations.

And, I was afraid because I don't know whom I can consider my friend anymore.

The person I exchange a friendly hello with most days, or offer water or cake to on a regular basis could be part of a terrorist cell plotting to destroy me or my family.

I haven't taken a self-defense class since middle school—and yes, that class was probably a joke anyway.

And although I did learn to shoot an M-16 when I was a teenager, I haven't a clue how to use a gun now, even if I were licensed to hold one.

Which I kind of want to be right now.

If I'm being honest.

Licensed to carry a gun.

Because I'm afraid.

Of what?

Losing my own life.

I knew I was stuck on fear, and when I was finally ready, I started to process.

I **stopped**, went out for a walk, and took some deep breaths. I noticed my tight shoulders begin to loosen as I continued to breathe and bring focus to them.

I **told** myself I was stuck on fear.

I **uncovered** one belief.

That there's a great chance I will get into a terrorist attack.

Is this 100% accurate? No.

This is where I got stumped. Consider other perspectives.

What?

Not be afraid?

That would be stupid and irresponsible.

So, what else is there to consider?

Tell myself: *Peace is around the corner?*

That would be naive.

But as time passed, and my fear became less intense, I came

up with one considerations that I was willing to take on.

I **considered** that life is ultimately out of my control. I can be as prudent as possible, but in the end, it's not in my hands. It's in Someone else's.

So, I chose to continue on with my life, perhaps with a little more caution than before, but otherwise more or less the same. I acknowledged that the emotion of fear might not leave me any time soon, though the fear of actually dying from a terrorist attack is fleeting.

I got stuck on fear, but it's **O.K**. It actually encouraged me to continue on with what my tradition commands me to do: Choose life and keep on living.

∼

The S.T.U.C.K. Method as a Life Practice

I implement The S.T.U.C.K. Method nearly every day of my life, because doing so empowers me to take control of challenging life situations and process through them in effective way. It is valuable in that it is at my fingertips when I get entangled in otherwise helpless situations. It offers me a reliable guide to expand my narrow thinking and encourages me to take on new ways of believing that I may not otherwise have considered. It consistently leads me to places of self-growth, transformation, and healing.

That said, it takes practice until The S.T.U.C.K. Method becomes a reflex. You will mess up sometimes, just like I do, and you may get discouraged. You may even question if The S.T.U.C.K. Method works. When that happens, remember that it is a **practice** and therefore is meant to be implemented over and over and over again, with the smallest of obstacles to the largest. It is a five-step method, not a five-minute lesson.

The S.T.U.C.K. Method is a life practice. With time, you may find that instead of you doing The S.T.U.C.K. Method, The S.T.U.C.K. Method is doing you. In other words, you may find yourself "stopping" when you are stuck on something or giving people the benefit of the doubt before you even realize you are processing through the steps of The S.T.U.C.K. Method.

Sometimes step **C—Consider** can be challenging and you may find it helpful to get assistance from an outsider. Ask someone, such as a confidante, a therapist, or a S.T.U.C.K. coach, to help you. I once asked for outside assistance from some friends to help me see new perspectives of a story that I may have otherwise been blind to.

Stuck on: Get Away from Here, You Beggar!

Last year, I noticed a beggar standing at a traffic light down the street from the entrance to my community.

How could I not notice her?

Covered from head to toe in a burqa and standing with a baby in her arms (even on the coldest days of winter), she would tap at my window, signing for money, nearly every day.

It was something you couldn't really miss or ignore.

I wondered to myself how much money she was earning from this "work."

You don't belong here.

Why are you begging so close to my home?

Why can't you stand somewhere farther, where I can't see you?

Why are you holding a baby?

Don't you know these severe cold temperatures and noxious fumes from the exhaust pipes can be dangerous for the infant?

Are you trying to elicit pity from your donors with the bundled baby?

That's probably part of your scheme.

This is making me very uncomfortable!

Who do you think you are, asking for money from people you don't even know?

You should get a job like the rest of us!

Why do you think you have a right to bother me?

There I was, stuck, and I knew it.

So, I started to process:

While at the red light, I **stopped**, closed my eyes for a moment, and took a breath.

I **told** myself that I was stuck on resentment.

I **uncovered** my beliefs and checked the accuracy of each of them.

I believed this woman didn't look like a beggar and she had no right to stand in such close proximity to my neighborhood.

I believed she was putting the newborn she carries when she "works" in danger and that she was making everyone that she approached uncomfortable.

When I reached the part to consider another perspective, I found myself not being able to move forward.

I couldn't see another perspective.

I did not want to invalidate the beliefs that still held true to me.

So, I reached out to a few friends for guidance who helped me realize the fallacies of my beliefs and come up with a list of other possible perspectives.

They helped me **consider** that there is no typical face of a beggar, that begging is income-earning work for some people, and that begging is not necessarily unrespectable. In fact, my friends reminded me that the Hebrew word for a beggar is "one who collects donations." In other words, this beggar could actually be enabling people to fulfill the commandment of giving donations to the needy.

Finally, they helped me see that I don't know the whole story. Perhaps this beggar is unable to hold down a job, or maybe she has a family member who is seriously ill and unable to work, or maybe she lives with an abusive husband who forces her to beg.

So, I chose to take the view that I didn't know the whole story and gave her the benefit of the doubt.

And from that place, I released the resentment I originally

had for her.

I got stuck on resentment and it's **O.K.**

Getting stuck actually helped me to broaden my narrow way of thinking and remind myself that I don't always know the whole story.

It also helped me to realize that if I ever come face to face with her or any other beggar, I don't have to be a slave to judgment but rather can be free to accept the unknown.

The more I practice The S.T.U.C.K. Method, the less I get triggered, in general. But, when I do get triggered, I find myself reacting more slowly and checking in with my beliefs sooner. I incorporate small shifts in my thinking and consider new perspectives, such as giving people the benefit of the doubt, reminding myself I don't always know the whole story, and cultivating gratitude with more ease instead of allowing a sticky situation to overcome me. In fact, I have found the more I consciously incorporate The S.T.U.C.K. Method into my life, the more I find myself implementing the method unconsciously, freeing myself from those overwhelming emotions, and moving on.

The work with The S.T.U.C.K. Method has opened my world up to possibilities for personal growth that I never knew existed. I have become more aware of the freedom that exists in the sacred space between a trigger and a reaction, and that I am not bound to function mindlessly. I have learned to recognize, too, this is a lifetime practice and I must take responsibility to continue choosing to do the work.

The S.T.U.C.K. Method is one way of getting out of life's sticky situations, and it is the way that works best for me in my life. Acknowledging I have practice opportunities at my fingertips, I aim to wake up to them every day to promote emotional well-being.

Acknowledgments

Stuck On: What If I Forget Someone?

A few days after I handed in the manuscript for this book to my editor for the last time, I sat down to write my acknowledgements.

I had already been walking around for days thinking about this task and feeling nervous about inadvertently leaving someone out. So to be prudent, I started writing myself notes whenever someone I wished to thank came to mind, so as not to be remiss in excluding them. Within a short time, I recognized my list had become very long. Besides including those who directly contributed to the creation of this book, I included friends, family, organizations, and religious and educational institutions that have impacted my life, as I recognized it was because of them I am the person I am today and hence, able to author this book.

Thank you to my parents, my husband, my children, my grandparents, my siblings, their spouses, my aunts, uncles, cousins, and 100+ people in the Taylor and Gura families, who provided endless unconditional love and support in my life and specifically during the writing of this book.

Thank you to my friends and teachers from Johnson Elementary School, Beck Middle School, and Cherry Hill High School East, who not only taught me about grammar and how to form sentences, but also challenged me to grow and think outside the box.

Thank you to my friends and teachers who supported my formal and informal early religious educations at Congregation Beth El, Camp Ramah in the Poconos, and

Hagesher U.S.Y. You guided me to experience and realize there is a world beyond the physical, and that such a world can be tapped into in a meaningful and joyful way.

Thank you to my professors, classmates, and colleagues in the psychology department of Rutgers University and in the occupational therapy department of Sargent College at Boston University. All of you supported my professional growth while I was on a journey I wasn't even aware I was on.

Thank you to my teachers and students at Integrative Yoga Therapy, Cherry Hill Health and Racquet Club, The Rohrer Center for Health and Fitness, and the JCC of Cherry Hill, NJ. The commitment you have to health and well-being inspire me to no end.

Thank you to the researchers, religious leaders, professors, and wellness coaches whose spiritual work, teachings, and writings continue to inspire me in my adult years.

Thank you to Nefesh B'Nefesh, for enabling my family to make the dream possible of moving to Israel, and to my Kibbutz Hannaton community, for making me feel at home even when I am thousands of miles away from my own family.

Finally, a big thank you to Julie Fisher, who introduced me to Three Gems Publishing, for without her, this book would not be in existence today.

Is that it?

Besides those who directly contributed to this book, am I missing anyone else?

Think, Shira, think! You can't leave anyone out!

Ah, my patient and understanding boss at Research Success Technologies, of course! How could I forget the person who gave me such leeway over the past year, while my attention and energy were focused on the writing of this book?

Is that it? Did I forget anyone else?

I wasn't sure.

So I set my acknowledgments page aside for a few days.

And then returned to it—when I wanted to express gratitude to my web designer, Sabrina Hall, who recreated my website with such wisdom, grace, and professionalism, and to Scott Alprin, Esq., the kindest, most patient, out-of-this-world, and generous trademark lawyer you will ever meet.

I guess that's it.

But I put the document aside again because I wasn't 100% confident I had everyone covered.

But I stood frozen.

Is this writer's block? I thought to myself.

No, silly, it's called being stuck!

So, I decided to **step away from the computer** and take a long walk in the woods near my house.

I checked in with what I was feeling and **told** myself I was stuck on fear.

So, I **uncovered** my beliefs.

I noticed I believed people will be very upset with me if I leave them out, and if that should happen, it's something for which I could never make up.

Really, Shira? Is that 100% accurate? Besides those who directly contributed to this book, who else do you think is expecting to be acknowledged? And even if you accidentally did leave someone out, do you really think they will be upset with you? You know there's always the possibility of expressing your thanks in person, and you could always update the book if need be.

Feeling a little better, I came up with a **consideration**.

I can consider that I did my best to create this acknowledgment page and doing my best is all I can ask of myself.

And so, I put my acknowledgments aside and began to write my thanks to those *who directly helped me with the creation of this book.*

I got stuck on fear, but it's **O.K.**

I am grateful I was able to catch myself and process through it.

To Those Who Directly Contributed to this Book

To my children: Ayalah, Aitan, Avi Chai, and Amir who granted me permission to write about them and attempted to be patient while I was working on my book. Thank you for continuing to love me unconditionally even when I get stuck.

To my husband, Boaz, who from day one said, "Go for it!" without the blink of an eye, who provided continuous support to our family so that I could take this project on, and, most important, who holds me in compassion when I get stuck. Always.

To my Jewish spirituality *Mussar* group. Thank you to Edite Birnbaum, Jamie Dollinger, and Shoshana Melman for creating this group with me, sharing your stories, and inspiring one another to bring more holiness into our lives. Your devotion, commitment, and support to this practice has offered me more insights into human nature, helped me recognize that transformation is possible, and provided me thoughts to ponder to deepen this book.

To my local Getting *un*STUCK group on Hannaton. Thank you to Anat Harel, Bebe Jacobs, Dorothy Richman, Hadas Almog, and Viki Langbeheim for your commitment to the weekly gatherings, your vulnerability with sharing your stories, and your strength to process through them. I am in awe of your dedication to self-growth and development, and the wise insights you offered to enhance this book.

To my graphic designer, Daniel Wolfsong. Thank you for your creative process and for remaining patient with me as ideas for the front cover and subtitles continued to evolve and change.

To my photographer, Yonit Matilsky-Tsadok. Thank you for your generosity and spontaneity in taking me on a walk one day to the Hannaton forest, which resulted in the beautiful photos for my website and book publicity. May you be blessed with continuing to enjoy your work and sharing your gifts with the world.

To my beloved aunt, Allison Taylor. I am grateful for your discipline and commitment to your own practice and for sharing your stories with me. Because of your own practice, you were able to offer wise and significant insights into this book, and for that I will be forever grateful.

Thank you to my editors, Jen Maidenberg, Arlene Plasky, and Sara Wildberger, for your wisdom, talent, and support. I feel blessed that you all chose to be a part of this team.

To my book coach and publisher, Esther Goldenberg, at Three Gems Publishing. When I began blogging several years ago, I never had any intention of turning my blog into a book. When I first learned about you, I sent a blind email not expecting to hear anything in return. Yet you responded—and with a sense of joy, excitement, and encouragement, all of which continued to sustain me throughout the entire process of putting this book together for publication. You had a vision for this book that I would never have been able to see on my own. Your work ethic, motivation, patience, creativity, positivity, strength, and wisdom are priceless. You came into my life as an unexpected gift. (If anyone reading this is even thinking about writing a book, I suggest you RUN, not walk, over to Three Gems Publishing!) This journey together has been powerful and transformative for me. From the depths of my heart, I thank you for it.

An Invitation to Share and Practice

Did this book make an impression on you? Do you have any thoughts or comments you'd like to share? **I'd love to hear from you!** You can email me at: shira@thestuckmethod.com

If you enjoyed this book, would you mind taking a minute to write a review on Amazon? It's actually quite easy if you are not familiar with it: You simply go into your Amazon account, click on "Orders" and then click on "Write a Product Review". Even if you received this book as a gift, you can still leave a review by scrolling down to the reviews on my book's page and write in your own. It does not have to be long and it would sure mean a lot to me. Thank you!

If you know of someone in your life that would benefit from reading this book, please send him or her a copy. You can purchase it on Amazon.com. If Amazon does not ship to your country, the book can also be purchased at Book Depository (www.bookdepository.com) and they ship nearly everywhere in the world! Thank you!

If you are interested in **organizing a "Getting *un*STUCK" presentation, workshop, or retreat** for your school, book club, community, place of worship, or company or would like to **order this book in bulk,** please contact me: shira@thestuckmethod.com. Thank you!

Finally, if you would like to **join the growing "Getting *un*STUCK" community** and receive weekly updates regarding practice opportunities for your own personal growth and many other fun stuff, you can sign up for my newsletter on the home page of my website. You can also like my Facebook page **(The S.T.U.C.K. Method)**, join my Facebook group **(Getting *un*STUCK)**, and follow me on Twitter and Instagram @thestuckmethod. Thank you!

References:

Kabat-Zinn, Jon. (1994). *Wherever You Go, There You Are: Mindfulness Meditation in Everyday Life:* Hyperion.

About the Author

Shira Taylor Gura is a well-being coach passionate about helping people get unstuck. She created The S.T.U.C.K Method by drawing on her training as an occupational therapist and yoga instructor. She leads workshops in environments ranging from corporate offices, to educational institutions, and community centers. Her belief that a more mindful, compassionate life is available to anyone, anywhere is reflected in her blog. She lives with her husband and four children on Kibbutz Hannaton in the Galilee, Israel.

Looking forward to getting *un*STUCK with you,

Shira

The S.T.U.C.K. Method™

www.thestuckmethod.com

35563326R00168

Made in the USA
San Bernardino, CA
28 June 2016